MY BIBLE OF BLUNDERS

first paperback edition 2019 ISBN: 978-1-927664-11-7
first clothbound edition 2019 ISBN: 978-1-927664-12-4

MY BIBLE OF BLUNDERS
Stumbling to Triumph in Business

Michael Friedman

cover art by Mariusz Zabdyr
layout by Veronica Roca

DISCLAIMER

The opinions and descriptions provided in this book are
exclusively those of the author and do not necessarily reflect those
of the editors and publishers at EnCompass Editions.

encompass
EDITIONS

MY BIBLE of BLUNDERS

Stumbling to Triumph in Business

Michael Friedman

encompass
EDITIONS

Mistakes, I've made a few, but one of my decisions is beyond criticism: the decision thirty-five years ago to ask Sindi Cohen to marry me has been responsible for most of my success and happiness. She has been an amazing wife and mother. I know it's a cliché, but Sindi has made me a better man and I owe most of my business success to her steady, quiet support.

My four boys — Ryan, Kevin, Adam, and Jonathan — bring me tremendous joy. They have always been on my mind when things got tough, and most of my hard work and financial success has been due to my love for them and my striving to provide them with better financial circumstances than I had. It's so cool to see what they've become: college graduates out in the world, working at jobs they care about.

This book is dedicated to all five of them, with love.

Mike

On the page following, I acknowledge people who've played a role in my career. Here, I'd simply like to thank two people who helped make this book happen.

Barry Mintzer, my very close friend. For the past 25 years we've spoken by phone every morning. His constancy in friendship has kept me in balance throughout my roller coaster career.

Robert Buckland, publisher at enCompass Editions, who served as my editor and claims to have enjoyed the process.

*

These are some of the people who, one way or another, for better or worse, helped shape who I am.

That's why I'm forever grateful to them all.

Coach Larry Shyatt	Director of summer Basketball League Cleve Hts 1968-1971 (Head Basketball coach at Wyoming/Clemson
Jim Cowan	Director of Recreation. City of Beachwood Ohio 1974-1978
Jim Hogan	Hillcrest YMCA Director 1977-78
Coach Bob Hamilton	Head Basketball Coach University of California Davis 1979-1980
Mark Termini	Sports Agent NBA Summer League 1982-1984
Coach Bill Sudeck	Head Basketball Coach Case Western Reserve U 1981-1983
Coach Herb Livsey	Director of Snow Valley Basketball Camp 1980-1982
Charlie Jones	Athletic Director Dyke College 1983-1986
Dale Zucker	CEO of Oracare 1986-1987
Mitch Marks	COO of Beachwood Security System 1988-1989
Bill Shoemacher	Athletic Director Beachwood High School 1988-1989

Michael Martella	CEO of Captain Tony's Franchisor 1989-1999
Mark Krinski	CEO of PC on Call 1998-1999
Bobby Ginn	CEO of the Ginn Companies 2000-2005
Jeff Davis	President of Ginn Sales 2000-2005
Dean Adler	CEO of Lubert Adler 2000-2019
Elva Pellachuid	CEO of Epiphany Luxury 2000-2019
Gary Waxman	CEO of WW Group Holdings 2005-2007
Scott Berkowitz	Partner with Destination Sales and REvision 2005-2012
Greg Perlman	CEO of GH Capital 20072009
Pablo Pinero	CEO and founder of Bahia Principe 2009-2010
Tom Morton	CEO of Denver division of Brookfield 2010-2011
Lamar Fisher	CEO of Fisher Auction/Mayor of Pompano Beach 2012-2013
George Perez	CEO of the Related Group 2012-2013
Greg Bankhurst	CEO of Dream Play 2013
Howard Schoor	CEO Chapin Estates 2012-2014
Greg Clement	CEO of Realeflow 2012-2013
John Domo	CEO of Domo Development 2013-2014
Justin Huff	CEO of Huff Grand Bakken Lodge 2013-2015
Nico Bolzan	President of Stark Capital 2014-2019
Frank Sinito	CEO of Millennia Companies 2014-2019

Content

To understand Michael Friedman, you need to appreciate the journey rather that the destination. His gift is his ability to take stock of current circumstances and pivot wholeheartedly to the next opportunity. He doesn't abandon the past with regret so much as embrace the future with boundless optimism. As a new business partner of Mike Friedman, I find both my writing and my personal interactions infused with his positivity. Without lecturing or philosophizing, this little book manages to touch on the age-old : loyalty to friends and family, an unfailing fortitude, the ability to get back on the proverbial horse.

We may sometimes wonder what we've actually learned in the course of our lives, what we've contributed. Friedman addresses these questions by sharing his tribulations, his challenges, and sometimes his triumphs. Unusually, he has the courage to admit how often he progressed through mistakes. His infectious optimism and desire to lift up others is his true talent and as his friend and colleague, my life has been enriched through knowing him. He never played in the NBA, but as a sportsman in the game of life, he emerges as a world-class all-star.

If you climb on the horse with Mike Friedman, you'll enjoy the ride.

David Hirsch

David Hirsch is a graduate of Cornell University and a serial entrepreneur in manufacturing, hi-tech, merchant banking and real estate development. He lives in Greenwich, CT.

THE MOVING
FINGER WRITES

If you're interested in business, I'm going to recount a few stories from my life and now and again I'm going to draw a few lessons from those stories. That's not to say I intend to lecture you constantly on your own professional life. This is not a "how to" book — you can tell that from the title — and it's not a "how not to" book either. But we can sometimes learn from our mistakes and occasionally we can learn from the mistakes made by others. Human circumstances and human experiences are so varied, it's hard to find road maps that match our own journeys. Still, we grow older and we gain the impression that we *are* learning, painful as the process is, and we'd love others to benefit from our stories if they could. Maybe you can spy a lesson here and there that I myself missed. In fact, judging from the number of times I've made the same mistakes, that should be easy.

I've had 41 jobs since I started working at fifteen as a warehouse boy stuffing fake eyelashes in boxes for a dollar an hour.[1] Some of those jobs — partnerships, ventures, escapades, whatever — have been pretty profitable and most of them have been entertaining at the least. *My Bible of Blunders* is so-called because I thought *My Song of Successes* would be less fun to read and maybe less useful. So this is my invitation to you to dip into my history for spare parts that may fit your own.

But wait a minute. Just before you start rummaging around in my mistakes, allow me to explain that I attended no business school, have no MBA and often fell asleep in economics class. Yet when I finally entered business I entered head first and without hesitation. This was possible because we humans have the ability to apply what we learn in one sphere of life to another sphere entirely. And believe me, my readers, I'd experienced full immersion in another sphere.

How the Ball Got in My Court

When I think about it, the toothbrush that looked like a baseball bat changed my life. I don't mean it made me rich or famous and it wasn't even my idea. But if I had to pick a thing that stood at the crossroads, that marked a major turn in a life that was to be filled with turns, it would be that toothbrush.

This of course demands some sort of explanation, which begins in Cleveland, Ohio, where I was born in 1955, the second child of Jerry and Charlotte Friedman. My older brother, Roger, was a clever and hard-working boy who excelled at school and collected coins as a hobby. My younger sister, Kathy, the baby of the family, was born 14 months after me. Mom was a housewife and Dad was a general contractor who worked for his brother's company for forty-five years and never complained. For me, being a kid was fun and I always thought we were

---

1   Arnie and Sydel Miller owned this operation, which evolved into Matrix Essentials, a shampoo company that sold for $1 billion in the 90s. Was that a good omen or what?

well to do since I lacked for nothing. Later on, I came to realize that we were just getting by, but by then the job of growing up was almost done.

Back to the explanation. We loved sports, my family. Roger and I were especially good at team sports and Roger and Dad became pretty impressive tennis players. It's hard to say exactly how my passion for basketball — not tennis or baseball — developed but it probably had its roots in my realizing I wasn't blessed with great intelligence or outstanding athleticism or brilliant family connections. If I was going to accomplish goals and realize dreams I was going to need outside guidance. That in turn probably had something to do with the way I was drawn to mentors and role models and teams. Dad was the first of these, my model for the right way to behave wherever I was, whatever I was doing. Maybe Barry Shamis, the boy next door, was also a role model, if an 11-year-old can be a role model. Barry loved the game of basketball and we played almost every day until I was fourteen, then both played on the middle-school team. I discovered I loved the competition but most of all I loved the idea of a team, and basketball was about five individual players trying to work together as one. As time went on, I realized I also liked to be the leader of the team and I took winning and losing seriously. I started studying the players and coaches who were not only good, but who like me really cared about winning.

Larry Shyatt was one of those. I met him when I was thirteen. He was six years older than me and was to become my first full-on mentor. Larry was small — 5'7" — but a great high school player. He coached our summer team and conducted basketball clinics. Today, people sometimes ask me why I don't drink or smoke or do drugs. I can't honestly say because I don't condemn people who do. But I do remember one afternoon fifty years ago when Larry was in charge of the summer basketball leagues in Cleveland Heights. I was in the 7th or 8th grade and guys my age were starting to experiment with alcohol and tobacco and marijuana. Larry knew I ran with the fast and the cool, as we were inclined to regard ourselves. That afternoon we'd stopped play for a break and he took me to one side of the baskets.

"Friedman," he said. "How you feeling today?"

"Fine, I think. Yeah. Fine."

"Good, good. Friedman, one thing. Athletes don't do drugs. At all."

I nodded.

"You know why?"

I shook my head.

"Because we don't need them." He let it sink in. "We're that good."

That one moment seems to have shaped my health choices for fifty years to come. Larry Shyatt went on to be a bench player at the College of Wooster and became a successful basketball coach, leading both Clemson and Wyoming as their head coach. Today, as I write, he's assistant coach at the Dallas Mavericks of the National Basketball Association.

When I was fifteen and in the 10th grade, my parents moved us from Cleveland Heights, Ohio to Beachwood, Ohio. I was shattered. It wasn't that I missed Cleveland Heights High School, it was the team and friends I'd expected to play basketball with … forever. How could I play for anyone else? But it was in fact basketball that provided the continuity and made the disruption bearable. From the perspective of all these years later, the move was probably an important building block in my character. I joined a new team and made new friends, and to this day kept both those friends and those I'd left behind.

And with that I embarked on a 16-year pursuit of the sport of basketball, a pursuit characterized by almost crazy conviction and perseverance. In the end it brought me to the toothbrush that looked like a baseball bat — but that must wait a few pages more.

I started college at Ohio University, transferred home to Cleveland State and moved on to the University of Arizona, where I earned a BSc diploma. During those years I never stopped playing, learning and coaching basketball, but the biggest — and most painful — thing I learned was that I was not a professional basketball player in the making. I swallowed hard and re-shaped my dream: I'd be a professional basketball coach.

The catch was that people didn't go from being recent college graduates saturated in basketball to professional college basketball coaches. If they did, they had family or friends in the professional ranks. If they didn't, they worked for years at the high school level. I couldn't see any of those options applying in my case so I took a job as a YMCA physical director at an annual salary of $8700 (that was subsistence money in 1977 too). Meanwhile I spent three months typing 314 letters to 314 U.S. colleges and universities and stuck on 314 13¢ stamps. I got four replies, all suggesting I try the high school level.

I mulled this perfect score for another year while I coached locally and worked at the Y. Then someone clued me into the fact that a query letter should say something like "I'm looking to earn my M.A. while working as a graduate assistant for your school's basketball program." I liked the ring of that so I wrote 331 new letters and mentioned some definitive times when I'd be in the recipient's city for a personal visit — as though I could be in 331 cities. This time just 290 schools didn't bother to respond, 34 schools said no thanks — and seven schools said they were interested. One response was a handwritten note from Bob "Ham" Hamilton, a well-known coach at University of California, Davis. Coach Hamilton said, yeah, he had an opening and he'd love to see me at his office on campus.

I started in Indiana, then flew to Kentucky, then flew to Baton Rouge, Louisiana, then to Salt Lake City Utah. The interviews seemed to go okay but nobody offered me a job. My last shot was the University of California, Davis. I flew to San Francisco, rented my first car, and drove to the campus. It was beautiful. I walked to the office at the gym. I realized I was hyperventilating a little. I slowed down, took a few deep breaths.

Coach Ham Hamilton was a man in his mid-50s who looked older. His dress was sloppy, his office a mess. There were five cartons of Lucky Strike cigarettes on his desk and a couple of bottles of antacids.

We talked basketball. Pretty soon the coach had me laughing and I could see that he could see that I had a ton of love for basketball and wasn't looking to be a star and didn't have any connections anyway. Finally he leaned back in his chair and waved his cigarette slowly in the air, the seventh cigarette of our meeting.

"So Michael, that's all great stuff, but what about your weaknesses? I don't just mean as a coach. I mean as a person too."

Man, I thought. I'm dead. He's seen right through me.

"Okay" I said. "I know. Like, my attire. I have to work on my attire. I'm color blind and don't know much about fashion."

Coach Ham burst out laughing. I don't know if I actually hung my head a little.

"I'm a bit of a slob sometimes," I mumbled.

Hamilton stopped laughing but I saw he was still smiling.

"Coach Friedman," he said. "You're hired. I've finally found somebody who'll make me look good."

For the next two years my actual job was sitting next to Ham on the bench. I hope I did make him look good but whether I did or not, I spent all my free time learning the game from this remarkably intense and likeable man. He was really my first exposure to genuine passion in sport. When the first play in the first game I witnessed went wrong, Ham rose from his seat and slammed his clipboard to the ground.

"God damn mother *fucker!*" he shouted. "We can't even win a fuckin' *jump ball?*" I looked at him in shock and awe. This man *cared* about the game. During the two years I watched him pace during games, and in our office later, I never saw him light a cigarette with a match. He always lit the next cigarette with the last. He didn't sleep after losses but walked the streets of Davis all night with a bottle and cigarette in hand. He was to die of lung cancer in 2013 and in 2015 they named the gym after him. I wish the old grouch had lived to experience the honor he so deserved.

But that first summer in California changed my professional life. Ham knew I was broke and wanted to reward me for my efforts. He arranged summer jobs for me as a basketball coach at various camps in Oregon and California. One of these turned out to be Magic Johnson's

In 1980 Hall of Fame and iconic basketball player and businessman
Ervin "Magic" Johnson and I posed for this photo at Johnson's first basketball
camp at Pepperdine University, Malibu, California.

first basketball camp at Pepperdine University in Malibu. Magic had just completed his historic rookie year, where he'd led the LA Lakers to an NBA championship over Philadelphia. He was already a sports celebrity and the camp had 450 campers. I brought my trademark enthusiasm and Magic appreciated it. We became friends and he told the owner of the camp, Max Shapiro, how much passion I'd shown.

Max asked me to work the next four weeks at different locations around Southern California. One of these was the Jamal Wilkes Camp at California State U, Santa Barbara, where by astonishingly good luck the National Cheerleading Camp was set up for the week. The ocean rolling in, the sandy beach, the cheerleaders, the counsellors, the basketball coaches, the toga party, the darkness of the long night. Once in a lifetime.

I'm not writing a book of self-praise here, but I have to tell you

*NBA Hall of Fame Jamal Wilkes and I at his
basketball Camp in Santa Barbara, California, 1980.*

that it was my popularity with the camp kids that prompted Max to extend camp coaching employment to me for the rest of that summer and the following summer. This was most of the California basketball camps — Magic Johnson, John Wooden, Jamal Wilkes, Phil Smith and Ron Lee — and almost without my realizing it, those two summers would be my first lessons in the power of networking and self-promotion, tools I seemed almost born to develop. And while it may sound corny, it was wonderful to be young and in California at that time. In 1980 and 1981 I'd become an assistant college basketball coach, attended graduate classes, and worked on my Master's thesis in sport psychology for a degree from California State U, Sacramento. I was on my own with no support and no financial help and almost no finances. I lived alone in a 700-square-foot apartment and that was fine with me. I waited on tables and played guitar two nights a week for ten bucks a night plus tips at a place called the Blue Mango. My social life in that era after the sexual revolution and before AIDS exceeded all my youthful dreams. I even fell in love, as young men should, and her name was Jane. Jane looked at me one night and her eyes were sad.

"Michael," she told me softly, "I can't keep seeing you."

"What? Seeing me? I'm right here!"

"It's the basketball, Michael. It's your life. You love basketball more than you'll ever love me."

"But," I protested. "But Jane … I love you more than *base*ball."

"I'll always remember that, Michael. Goodbye."

She broke my heart.

Here I am at the UCLA camp with Hall of Fame coach Pat Riley of the LA Lakers, the NY Knicks, the president of the Miami Heat and NBA champion as a player and six times as a coach.

Now came the hard part. The summer of 1981 was ending and I needed a real — properly paid — job as an assistant coach. By now I'd made connections in the sport but there were few openings and before I seriously pursued any of those, I went home for my sister Kathy's wedding. While I was there I bumped into the head coach at Case Western Reserve, a strong academic college right there in Cleveland, one with a weak basketball program. Bill Sudeck had held the position for 30 years and right away he started selling me hard on the virtues of coming home. Then to my astonishment, he offered me a job — head assistant coach. I managed to get over my amazement long enough to accept the offer and went on to negotiate an additional role as founder and manager of a new summer basketball camp to be called the Spartan Basketball Camp. It was to remain in operation for another 26 years.

Atendees at the Spartan Basketball Camp, founded by me in 1981 and seen here in its second year, 1982. The camp brought together hight school and college coaches from around the USA and operated for 31 years.

I was back home and surrounded by friends and family. I loved it. Yes, I had to swallow hard when I learned that my salary as a first assistant coach at a Division-3 school was $2500 a year but I resolved to make a 110% effort regardless. I simply took five other jobs to pay the bills. Nothing to it.

- Up at 5:30 to supervise the new jogging track at my old high school from 6:00 to 8:30 every morning Monday to Saturday. They paid $8 an hour.
- Change clothes to suit and drive downtown to work as outside sales guy for a buddy's t-shirt printing business He paid $2.13 an hour plus commissions.
- Change clothes to teach phys-ed from 12:30 to 2:30 at a Jewish elementary school. Little bastards were tough and there was no discipline.
- Drive three days a week to inner-city Glenville High to teach driver's education.
- Drive to real job as assistant coach at Case Western and conduct practice from 4:00 to 6:00.
- Dinner at fast-food joint.
- Change to basketball officiating clothes and drive to armature basketball league games anywhere in the city. Paid $15 cash per game.

A few months had passed since my return to Cleveland and I was making some attempt to recapture my California lifestyle — impossible with six jobs but I was game to try. At a downtown club one night in June of 1982 I saw a young woman whose brothers I'd coached in the seventies. Her name was Sindi Cohen and she looked across the room at me and lit up the place with a billion-dollar smile. A few days later we went out together for the first time and I was in love.

"I'm not sure I totally understand your basketball thing," she said to me one evening when we'd been dating for almost two years.

"Ah," I said. "But I love *you* more than basketball."

Got it right that time. We married in 1985 and have four terrific sons.

Bill Sudeck was a living legend at Case Western Reserve. He'd been the basketball coach there for over 35 years and he was also the cross-country and track coach. His record in basketball was lousy, but his record in track was fantastic, and his players loved him. A lot of successful doctors, lawyers, and business leaders were strong supporters of Coach Sudeck. The man taught me that "if you love what you do, then you never have to work a day in your life." He actually believed he was at play every day, and he loved it, loved working with student athletes.

"Look," he told me. "These student athletes at Case are some of the smartest and most motivated young academics in the U.S. Most of them are in pre-med or pre-law or in the six-year engineering programs."

"But don't they care about the game?" I was channelling Coach Hamilton.

"Mike, you gotta understand what these Division-3 non-scholarship players are really in school for. Winning on the court is good but it's a distant second to winning in life."

Me, I'd always hated the opposing coach, but Sudeck would actually invite the winning coach to dinner and everybody would drink and eat and have a great time. It started to sink in for me that our competitors were just like us. They might even be people we'd meet and work with later. They might even be part of our network!

Coach Sudeck has been dead almost twenty years now but I like to think his humor and wisdom is still part of me.

My two years at Case Western — including the Spartan Basketball Camp —were a success for me and they were capped when a former Sudeck player and friend of mine, Mark Termini, asked me to coach in the NBA Summer Basketball League in Los Angeles. I was 26-years-old and invited to coach players who were in the NBA or trying to make the NBA — among the best players on planet earth. That season was to remain one of the greatest thrills of my life and my win-loss record was 6-2. As a bonus, I learned an indirect, sad, important lesson.

John Wiley, at 6'9, was a star player at the University of Minnesota and the best on my teams. It maybe wasn't such a huge surprise when Pat Riley, the assistant coach of the LA Lakers, called me up and asked if he could come to my practice and watch John Wiley play. I felt a twitch of excitement and asked why.

"Well, I might possibly ask him to play with our team and maybe get a chance to play in pre-season with the Lakers. You know, give the kid a chance to make the team as a free-agent rookie."

"Holy smokes," is all I said.

Our practice started at 10:00 a.m. sharp and Coach Riley was there. We chatted for a few minutes while we waited. John Wiley never showed.

"John! John! That you?"

"Uh, who's this?"

"It's Mike Friedman. Where are you?"

"Uh, in bed?"

"John, this was a once-in-a-lifetime opportunity to play for the Lakers and you overslept?"

"Guess I did."

I never forgot this — in basketball or after. Be prepared, be ready and most of all — *show up!*

Word had gone out that local Dyke College, which also had a truly terrible basketball record, was looking for a head coach — a savior in other words. Dyke had an enrollment of only 97 men and 450 women — mostly inner-city Cleveland students — but had been founded 90 years earlier and graduated the likes of Harvey Firestone and John D. Rockefeller. Eighty applicants had applied for the position but I had to try and now my pattern of making and holding close friendships began to bear fruit. My colleague Rip Taylor had been coaching overseas and now went to the athletic director's office in person to recommend me. The athletic director was African American and Rip was African American and most of the students were inner-city African Americans, yet here was Rip commending a white suburban kid not only as a coach and teacher, but as a person who would inspire these inner city players. Ervin "Magic" Johnson and Pat Riley, then head coach of the NBA champion LA Lakers, also called in with personal recommendations. I became the youngest college basketball head coach in the state of Ohio. I was 28.

I was to spend three happy years at Dyke in this position as well as part-time professor, moonlighting basketball official and athletic director. My record for those years was 46 wins to 29 losses, which made me the winningest coach in Dyke College history.

And it was during those years at Dyke that something began to shift. I was working 80 and 90-hour weeks and although my third-year salary was $29,000, Sindi and I would talk about the future.

"I still don't totally get this basketball thing," she reminded me. "You're struggling for what?"

Hmm. I began to wonder if a young man who could bootstrap himself in the basketball world with nothing going except hunger and passion couldn't bootstrap himself otherwise. What about business for instance? My reputation in the business world was spotless because, after all, I'd never been in business. And didn't everybody love sports and success and wasn't I a successful sports guy?

Surely team building and management were my strengths. I embarked on a campaign of job applications and interviews that was about as dogged as my earlier search for a coaching position. That seemed so long ago now.

Going to Bat for Myself

"Mike?" My dad was calling. As so often, he had my back. "Mike, my friend Joel has a friend. Guy named Dale. He's been a pretty successful lawyer but he's gone into business — some sort of sports marketing business — and I guess he needs a sales manager. Joel thought you might like to meet him."

Sports marketing? Sales manager?

"Give me his number, Dad."

The sign on the office door in suburban Cleveland said ORACARE. The office itself a modest, third-floor premises. Dale was on the phone. He was a short, well-dressed guy about 5'7" and looked about 35 years old. He waved to a chair and kept talking. When he was done he scribbled something on a pad. I introduced myself and we exchanged pleasantries. At a certain point he opened a drawer, took something out, set it on the desk. We both looked at it for a long moment.

"Ever seen one of these?" he asked me.

"Yeah. Yeah, I have."

"What is it?"

"Well, it looks to be a baseball bat for a very small player, somebody maybe a foot tall."

Dale looked up. "Ha ha," he said. "Good."

He picked up the bat and twisted one end.

"It's a toothbrush," he said.

"Wow."

"Listen, Mike. My best friend Ruben is a dentist. He told me the toughest thing he and every dentist faces is getting kids to brush their damn teeth."

"Okay. I get it. Every kid loves baseball. That's a great idea, Dale."

"Sure, Mike. But it's not *the* idea. See, this is a *Yankees* baseball bat and this is the Yankees team logo. So we're not marketing cool toothbrushes, we're marketing the Yankees!"

I was in awe.

"And every other team that pays us!"

"That's fantastic, Dale!"

"Patent pending, my friend."

And so I turned a corner in life and entered the world of business. Dale and his partners hired me as their national sales manager and I in turn recruited and managed 85 independent sales reps across the U.S. The bat was licensed by the NBA, the NFL, by Major League Baseball and by college groups across the country. We sold to drug stores, toy stores, grocery stores. We had over a million little bat brushes sold in our first year and I made twice as much money as I'd ever made. It was clear, however, even to a novice such as I was, that the venture was under-capitalized and chasing new money consumed a great deal of management time. You could tell this was so since vendors called every few days searching for their money and yelling at whomever was unlucky enough to have answered the phone.

Dale himself was dynamic and charismatic and exhibited three personality characteristics that I came to recognize in certain entrepreneurs over the years to come. 1. He had mental blinders on that prevented him from seeing short-term problems or setting short-term goals. 2. He suffered from some sort of attention deficit disorder when communicating with employees. 3. He possessed acute long-distance mental goggles that allowed him to see only where the company was headed and the pot of gold that waited there. He had a few flaws too.

It was early in my second year with the company. I'd been ten days on the road, traveling with our new sports reps, and was back in the office in Cleveland. The phone rang but the secretary wasn't around so I answered. It was our product manufacturer (and principal investor), Bob Sekine, calling for Dale from New York. I told him Dale was out on a business trip.

"Business trip, is he? Know where?"

"I'm afraid I don't. Can I take a message?"

"Who would I be speaking to?"

"I'm Mike Friedman, the national sales manager."

"Oh yes, Mr Friedman. I've been hearing about you. Doing quite a job, they tell me."

"Thank you, sir. Thank you very much."

"Enjoy selling, do you?"

"Well, we've sold a million brushes since I joined the company. I'm pretty proud about that."

"And how long have you been with Oracare, Mike? Can I call you Mike?"

"Oh sure. About a year now."

"Well that's great. It certainly is. Mike, look, you strike me as a likable guy and you sure as hell gotta be working hard."

"Thank you, Mr Sekine."

"So I'm going to make a recommendation to you. That all right?"

"Of course, Mr Sekine."

"I'm going to recommend that you resign immediately."

I stood with the phone in my hand for what must have been a very long moment.

"Why?" I finally asked.

"Because your boss is a liar and he's dangerously close to getting himself in serious trouble."

There was another silence.

"Liar," I eventually repeated. "Serious trouble."

"That's right. Just a recommendation, mind you. You can mention it to Dale if you like — or not. I don't really care. But tell him I called. And Mike, congratulations on your good work."

I didn't resign immediately but I did start listening more carefully to office gossip and paying closer attention to Dale himself. I had to admit that, in addition to his other qualities, the man was erratic, anal, and, er, not a nice guy.

Finally, some time in 1987, I started to feel really vulnerable and compromised. I began to make inquiries and a security firm offered me a position as a sales director. At the same time, my alma mater offered me a position as head high school coach. It was time to say goodbye to Oracare.

I went in to see Dale personally to give him my two-weeks notice. He looked at me for a moment with something like frank malice.

"I'm glad you're resigning," he finally said. "I was going to fire you next week anyway."

Oh right. I was the only sales professional he'd had, and I'd been kicking ass for him to the tune of a million baseball bat toothbrushes. Oracare went out of business eight months later. I hear Dale went to prison in Texas.

And yes, I would indulge in a last delightful year of coaching at my old high school, but the moving finger had writ, as the poet says, and there was no erasing it. I had entered the world of business.

I Learn While I Burn: Lesson 1

Every mistake is a brilliant move in disguise

Every person is entitled to a few mistakes. I for example devoted fifteen years to a poorly paid profession in a field unrelated to my ultimate career. I made a blind leap into the dark when I went to work for a criminal. Hey, that's three mistakes, isn't it?

But blunders are only blunders when they have no silver lining and these early blunders were all lining. From my years in college basketball I learned a tremendous amount about human relationships and the value of cultivating them. The poor pay was the reverse side of passionate and fulfilling choices. And the leap in the dark was also a leap into cold water. This, I realized, was a world of sink or swim and I was going to swim.

Not all my lessons would be so painless.

*

THE CAPTAIN'S TALES

The spring of 1989 was a warm one in Cleveland and the doors of Captain Tony's Gourmet Pizza were often open onto Shaker Square. The square itself is quite attractive today — the trees have filled out well and the store fronts are generally pretty toney — but in 1989 the neighbourhood was barely scraping through. Dick Kretch was the father of one of my best friends and a seasoned real-estate veteran. "It may be your dream, Mike," he told me when I pitched him my exciting plans, "but it's a dream destined to fail. Please don't open in Shaker Square."

"Why not?"

"Location, Mike, location. Nothing more to say."

I ignored Dick's advice just as I ignored almost everybody's. I was a thirty-four-year-old man whose lifetime career to that point had been as a successful basketball coach. I was a clear winner. Sure, my knowledge of the food industry started and stopped with eating food, but why shouldn't people take seriously my plans to launch a local chain of specialty pizza restaurants?

The lunch hour was just shifting into gear that morning and already Captain Tony's was buzzing, buzzing as it had been since we'd opened in March. The place was filling with the smells of tender baking crust and garlic and herbs and bubbling mozzarella. The sleek black and red booths were filling with hungry customers and my team — a man with fifteen years of coaching behind him could only think in terms of teams — was looking smart in their black pants and red shirts — bright, motivated and crackling with enthusiasm. Or so I hoped. I was certainly right there with them, encouraging them, helping them, greeting our customers as they arrived, making sure everyone was happy, all the time keeping an eye on our take-out operation on the other side of the space.

About 11:30, Sherman Leavitt arrived. I can still picture him standing in the doorway in his blue blazer and red tie and gray slacks. As usual he was puffing a bit, being a pretty heavy-set guy maybe twenty years my senior and diabetic. And as usual his forehead was damp with perspiration.

"Sherman!" I called. My arms were full of paper towels or something. "You're early, Sherm! We're just starting to look after the mob!"

"No problem." As always, his expression somehow managed to be both serene and worried at the same time. He waved his hand. "I just wanted to see this place run. No problem."

"Hey, Sherm. Look, grab that little table at the back and take in the scene. Soon as the numbers die down, we're gonna talk. Want a coffee?"

"Yeah. Yeah. Great. No sugar."

"Andrew!" I'd just hired this kid the week before, "Andrew, get Mr Leavitt a coffee, no sugar."

"Actually, I will have a sugar, Mike." Sherman lumbered to the back of the room. "Two, actually."

"Andrew!" I called. "Make that two sugars for Mr Leavitt. He's our accountant. Gotta look after this man."

Sherman was the father-in-law of one of my best friends and for twenty years he and his partner had operated a successful accounting firm specializing in small business. But when I first came to him, wild-eyed with enthusiasm but clearly short on capital, he'd offered to work for a small percentage of the business until I had enough cash flow to pay his quarterly bills. And maybe on account of that or maybe because he simply cared about his clients, he'd begun to mentor me about the many aspects of business I'd managed to avoid knowing anything about.

"Sure you're okay, Sherm?" I called.

He smiled from his table at the back.

"Fine," he said. "But your coffee's strong. Maybe one more sugar?"

As we know, I'd been a basketball coach for fifteen years and I'd been a good basketball coach too. But at a certain point I'd experienced one of those epiphanies that seems to crop up in the lives of budding entrepreneurs. It's like the pressures that build up underneath the earth and nobody notices until one day there's a tipping point and — boom — the world rocks. My world rocked when I realized, hey, I didn't like working for other people. No matter how much I loved the work and no matter how much I contributed, I was always contributing to someone else's creation. As things turned out, I was often to work for other people, but I was ready at all times to go it alone. It's like I was a peaceable sheriff, but I carried a six-shooter in my holster just in case.

This is going to sound hokey, but it all started changing during conversations with an Italian kid who worked in a pizza joint. Ken was one of my players when I was athletic director at Dyke, the inner-city college in Cleveland, and the two of us loved to talk pizza. I told him how, when I'd been coaching in the NBA Summer Basketball League in Los Angeles a few years earlier, Spagos and California Pizza Kitchen and their "gourmet" pizzas were all the rage. Why, I wondered to Ken, couldn't I bring that phenomenon to Cleveland?

I resigned a temporary job as a sales manager and started prowling through the microfilm files of food industry publications at the local library. Here I uncovered two facts that set fire to my fledgling ambition. First, pizza was one of the few food types at that time that lent itself to home delivery. (Shockingly, this is still somewhat true today.) Second, pizza rated third in 1988 among all fast foods, behind only hamburgers and fried chicken. And the authors noted (correctly as it turned out) that increasing health concerns would favor the baked pizza over its fried competitors.

So what should be my first step? Wasn't I supposed to create some business plan thing? I didn't know much about business plans because we generally didn't use them in basketball and anyway, they didn't sound like fun. But wait — wasn't original research important? Who actually did make the best pizza in America?

In the spring of 1988, I said goodbye to my wife, Sindi. I'd packed a sleeping bag and a few changes of clothes.

"Where will you stay?" a bemused Sindi asked as I kissed her goodbye at the door.

"In the car. Don't worry. I'll call every night."

I started down the sidewalk.

"What if it rains?" she called.

"Don't worry. I'll roll up the windows."

I threw my little suitcase in the trunk of the brown Comet I'd inherited from my grandfather.

"What will you eat?"

"Pizza!"

I set out from our little house in Cleveland and headed west to California and then back through Colorado to St Louis and then on through Kentucky and up to Chicago. At every opportunity I stopped and ordered whatever the locals said was the best pizza in town. It was tiring and fattening but also amazing fun. It was as though all of America was stitched together by a network of pizza. Like the country, the ingredients sounded similar but the results were distinctive and it goes without saying that I'd soon refined my pizza palette to a remarkable degree. I knew my doughs, I knew my cheeses, I knew my pepperonis and I knew my tomato sauces.

During my long hours at the wheel, I had plenty of time to chew over the reading I'd done at home. I knew that 93% of independent restaurants fail in the first year and even for me, with nothing to lose and bursting with confidence, that was scary. Before I was out of California I'd started wondering what I was going to learn from places that would be out of business by December. I began to focus on franchise operations because the failure rate for franchises was only 11%. My strategic basketball brain took over here. I knew I was good but I wasn't perfect. If I was going to improve my chances of winning, I needed some sort of proven system. Of course that was what franchises were all about. So I visited fancy pizza eateries, I visited mom-and-pop outfits, I visited outlets of the big chains. Not all of them were well known but they were all franchises, large or small.

On July 19th, 1988, after 12 days on the road, I pulled into New York City. The first night, I met a guy who ran a pizza joint next to the little hotel I found on 42nd. Street (I'd decided not to spend the nights in the car in Manhattan.) I explained my mission to him.

"No, buddy," he said, sort of kindly. He dropped a paper plate in front of me. "No no no no. You're in the wrong part of the state."

"What?" I must have looked shocked. "New York City? Wrong for pizza? You kidding? Didn't the mafia invent pizza here or something?"

Even as I asked, I was biting into my slice. The crust was a little leathery.

"Look." My host leaned on the counter. It turned out his name actually was Mario. "You said gourmet pizza, right? That means good, right?"

"Gotta be the best in America," I said, meanwhile making it clear I was really enjoying chewing on his product.

"Rochester," Mario said.

"Rochester." I nodded, chewing. "Kodak Rochester?"

"The best."

"How could that be?"

"Well, it's us Italians, ain't it? There's more Italians in Rochester, per capita, like, than anywhere in the state. All them wives and mamas are makin' their homemade sauces an' dough an' all. There's like a friendly war going on between them and the restaurant cooks."

New York is a big state but I pulled into Rochester early that same evening. Right away in a motel lobby I picked up a copy of something called Rochester Magazine and I was pretty astonished to open it to a list of the best pizza shops in town. Must be a sign, I figured. I read down. For the sixth straight year, it said, Captain Tony's Pizza and Pasta Emporium was Number One. I flipped through the yellow pages, jumped in the Comet and headed straight over to one of their franchised locations, on Monroe Boulevard. I ordered a Five Cheese and a Primavera.

Incredible.

Over the next two days, I asked everybody in town. People would see me coming and call, "Hey! Pizza Man!" But everybody agreed Captain Tony's was the best. The next day I ordered the Classic and the Seafood. On the third day I tracked down Michael Martella, owner.

The man was a little guy but fast talking and passionate.

"It's a sort of passion, Mike." He actually leaned forward in his chair as he said this. "I've got to bring great pizza — my great pizza — to this whole country. Rochester? I own Rochester, but I've just hired a consultant — and he doesn't come cheap — and this guy knows franchising. Captain Tony's going nationwide."

I liked this man. I liked his *feeling* — it was a lot like my own.

"So, Michael," I told him after I'd sketched out my own vision, "you've just met the man who's going to bring Captain Tony to Cleveland — and beyond."

"That's you?"

"Yes it is."

He looked at me very sternly. Then he smiled.

"I like you, Mike. I like your *feeling*. I even like your name."

"I'm ready to go, Michael."

"Okay. I believe you. I believe you could carry the Cleveland flag for the Captain."

"You bet I can!"

"So all's you need's the money and the experience."

"Right you are, Michael. Well, actually, those are the two things I don't have — yet. But believe me, Michael, I'll get them both soon."

He was quiet for a minute. This was, after all, his baby we were talking about.

"The franchise fee's twenty thousand bucks, Mike," he finally said.

"I'll get it."

"And you're going to need two hundred thousand to set up a classy operation like you're talking about."

"I'll get it."

"I'm sure you will. And the experience — well, I can help with that. But the passion, that's got to come from you."

"I just drove two thousand miles looking for you, Michael."

He nodded.

"Yeah. See your point, Mike. See your point."

So in the end we agreed I'd pay $10,000 of the $20,000 fee upfront as soon as I'd put together the financing. We shook hands and I left with one of the Captain's newly developed BBQ Chicken pizzas — large. It was a four-hour drive from Rochester to Cleveland and I hardly noticed.

If I arrived back home in triumph, it only required a few days for reality to bite. It was easy to contact real estate brokers and ask them to look out for a suitable location. But there remained the little problem of

$200,000 — or $220,000 to be exact. Clearly my plans had to include a visit to my local banker. And if I didn't know much, I did know that banks were leery of financing restaurant deals, since so many failed, even those well capitalized and run by experienced restaurateurs. I had this queasy feeling that the bankers might hold it against me that I had exactly no restaurant experience or business experience of any sort and that I had no money or collateral of any sort. On the other hand, I had boundless confidence and chutzpah. That had to count for something, right?

I made eight enthusiastic presentations to eight bankers and, on the basis of my lively presentation skills, I received two offers to go into banking and eight swift and unconditional rejections of my loan applications.

I moped around the house for a couple of days before finally returning to the drawing board. If the bankers could resist my pitch, there must be people out there who couldn't. These would be my family and friends, I reasoned.

Our place was small, so my father agreed we could use his home. I bought a bunch of frozen pizzas and invited everybody I knew. To my tremendous relief, nineteen showed up. Four were relatives and fifteen were acquaintances. We sat around for a while and chatted over coffee until I got up, took a deep breath, and turned to my flipchart. There was no PowerPoint in 1988.

I was totally innocent of offer memoranda, executive summaries, underwriters and internal rates of return. Anyone could see my presentation was based on a passionate dream and the excitement of launching a new venture, but when I looked around the room, this excitement wasn't reflected in the eyes of my little audience. I started to experience frustration. A few people did ask questions, but they were about financial issues. Financials? I was talking about taking the country by storm here.

At that point, the oven bell went off and we adjourned for pizza. I don't know if these people had all missed dinner or what, but they tore into those hot pizzas and pretty soon everybody was laughing and talking, You'd think I'd served them vodka martinis instead of store-bought pizzas. "Listen, friends," I said. "You like this pizza? This pizza is nothing compared to the gourmet pizzas our chefs will be making for our customers. Nothing!"

I sensed the buzz was positive and seized the moment.

"Folks," I said, looking into their eyes, now alert above cheerfully chewing mouths, "Folks, I know you all know me, and you know how hard I work and will work for you and your investment. But I only want you to invest an amount that you're one hundred per cent comfortable losing. As much as I know this venture will succeed, I want you to understand that even if it failed, I must remain in good standing as your friend and family member. Nothing must put that at risk."

By 8:45, when I bid good-night to the last of my guests, I had funding commitments for $225,000 and within a week, a young real estate broker had found me a location in a depressed area of inner Cleveland: Shaker Square.

It was 1:30 before the lunchtime crowd began to thin out and I finally joined Sherman at the back table. Who knows how many coffees and sugars he'd worked through by then? I ordered us a couple of slices of a Hawaiian that was already out of the oven. I sat down. I knew the guy had to be impressed by what he'd seen.

"So?" I asked.

Sherman nodded because his mouth was full.

"It's a gold mine, right, Sherm?"

He nodded again but raised his eyebrows at the same time.

"What I love, Sherm, is that every person who walks in that door is another fistful of dollars for Captain Tony."

"Revenue," Sherman said a bit indistinctly.

"Right. Revenue for Captain Tony. And I'm the guy who can

keep them walking in. Every day. And not just here but soon other locations too."

Sherman sat back and looked at me with that placid but worried expression of his.

"Revenue and expenses for Captain Tony, Mike."

"Right. Right," I repeated. "Revenue and expenses." I took a bite of the Hawaiian. The ham was a teeny bit too salty. I made a mental note to talk to Lou in the kitchen.

"Mike." Sherman dropped his tone just a fraction. "I know you've been monitoring your food and wages bills, right?"

" 'Course, Sherman."

"What do you think about your projected debt servicing costs?"

"Um. Good. Good."

"My profit and loss statements?"

I put down my slice. "Look Sherm. You know I never trained in accounting and I never took any business courses. You know I trained in psychology and physical education. I understand people and motivation, not numbers. That's why I need experts like you. But I do know how to get people to walk through this door and call this phone number and the more people walk in and call, the more money I make."

Sherman nodded, but slowly.

"This pizza's good, Mike."

"Thank you, my friend."

"Mike, let me ask you one question. If you had to choose, which would be more important to you, customers and sales — or costs?"

"Come on, Sherm." I laughed. "You know me. Of course it's my customers and my sales. That's why we're already doing so well here. I'm great with my customers and that's why they buy my pizzas."

Sherman finished off his slice and chewed the last bite slowly.

"Okay," he said, moving in even closer. "How about this idea: You're dead wrong."

I laughed again, a bit nervously. "How could I be wrong?"

"You're wrong because you're not in business to see how many mouths you can feed. You're in business to make a profit and a profit is what's left after you subtract your costs from your revenue. Costs always trump sales."

"Nah."

"It's true, Mike." He smiled for the first time. "Keep an eye on that bottom line. And while you're at it, be thinking about your exit strategy."

"I don't need an exit strategy, Sherm. I'm going to open another Captain Tony's — and real soon. And then another and another."

"Well maybe you are, young Mike. I hope you are. And I hope you can keep an eye on them all and I hope you're not still spinning pizza dough when you're ninety-five."

"I'm thirty-three and I'm on top of the world."

"I just want to keep you there, Michael."

"I know you do, Sherm. But I've got the vision. I've got the drive. That's what makes business. You keep adding up those numbers and I'll keep bringing in the cash."

I remember him looking at me with that serene expression of his. Serene and worried at the same time — that was Sherman Leavitt.

*

It was the morning of the 16th of May, and the young trees in Shaker Square were in full leaf and Captain Tony's was in full bloom. We were well into the new decade and I'd entered a new phase of my life.

Dawn Biachi started out in the kitchen cutting pizzas, but she'd proved so energetic and competent, I'd soon made her our controller and general manager. My brother-in-law Michael Cohen came aboard to help with marketing and he and I set fire to the business. We mailed out a Captain Tony's newsletter. We created hundreds of corporate accounts for local Cleveland offices, who then became priority customers. We started hand delivering to our top-100 corporate clients individual chocolate "pizzas" with candy "pepperoni" accompanied by hand-written thank-you notes. Our "Post-It" campaign attached to the front doors of homes $3 coupons that looked like UPS delivery notes. And because we appreciated that our most powerful promotional tool was word of mouth, I'd spend half an hour every day drilling into my team the golden rule: Treat our customers as we'd like to be treated ourselves.

For these reasons and others, by that spring everybody on the East Side of Cleveland was talking about Captain Tony's. We'd opened up two more locations and had lines out the doors on Friday, Saturday and Sunday evenings. Our ability to keep up with the crowds was thus far just average, so I was doing damage control by working the room, giving out free bread sticks, discounted wine, and slices of pizza. Some evenings I hired a magician to entertain the hungry crowds. I was working seventy-five hours a week running back and forth between the three locations and even though I was eating "America's Finest Gourmet Pizza", I'd lost twenty-one pounds. It was the spring of 1991 and Captain Tony's Gourmet Pizza in Cleveland was taking in two million dollars a year.

I never cared for paperwork but by now I had an office so I could look after it in peace. On the morning of 16th May, 1991, there was a soft knock on the door. It was Dawn Biachi. She sat down in the only chair apart from my own. This was not something she normally did.

"Mike." There was something about her tone. "Mike, I think we may have a little problem. I'm not sure — I mean, maybe we don't have a problem but it looks like we do."

"Is it Andrew?" I asked. The kid had been with us since our second month, but he was hard to motivate. They all were, really, but I'd made motivating — and retaining — my staff a specialty. Turnover was the bane of the restaurant business, as I'd learned.

"No no. He's fine. It's our money."

"Our money? What's wrong with it?"

"It's gone."

"You're out of checks, you mean?"

"No, Mike. I mean we're out of money."

I just couldn't understand what she was saying.

"Dawn, Captain Tony is taking in two million bucks a year."

"I know, Mike. But maybe Captain Tony is spending two million and one bucks. I don't know, Mike. I'm not an accountant. But we can't make the payroll or pay any suppliers because there … there just isn't any money."

I don't think I said anything for a minute. Then I roused myself.

"I'll call Sherman," I said.

Sherman Leavitt looked up from a mess of papers spread across his desk. I was in his place now.

"Mike Mike Mike," he said. "I'm sorry to see this."

"Is it fatal, Sherman?"

"Well, it's never fatal in business. All you need is enough money and the patient recovers right away."

"Yeah, but it looks like it's money I don't have."

"Hmm." He studied a ledger with "Capt Tony" on the cover. "I haven't seen these for months but everything appears in order. You don't seem to have spent all your profits on gambling or drink. You seem to have spent them on advertising, marketing, food waste, employee theft and a whole bunch of other worthy causes." He looked up. "Why did you do that?"

I swallowed hard.

"I didn't notice?"

"Sadly, I believe you. So now what are you going to do, Mike?"

"I thought you might tell me."

"I'm an accountant not an entrepreneur."

"Okay." I looked at my shoes awhile. "So I'm the entrepreneur but it's promoting and selling I'm good at."

"Right. Well then, promote and sell the fact that you're a good bet as a borrower. Remember Mike, you've got excellent cash flow. You've had that since day one. You simply failed to contain your costs. And costs are ... what?"

I smiled grimly. "More important than sales, right?"

Sherman nodded. His expression was serene, but worried.

"Right," he said.

Of course a business as seemingly successful as ours had access to a line of credit and considerable goodwill. The only issue was overcoming the perception that we had "millions" in the bank. I drew on the line of credit, needless to say, but this wasn't enough. I had to go to each of our vendors — food and packaging suppliers — and ask them for time. It was humbling to say the least. We of course had no choice about paying our employees and the government insisted upon their share but that left our rent and utilities hanging out for months. There was nothing to do except be totally transparent with our creditors and get back to work.

Dear Sherman Leavitt died ten years ago from complications arising from diabetes. He haunts me still.

I Learn While I Burn: Lesson 2

Numbers count

I think I probably learned more about business from my ten years as the owner of six Captain Tony's eateries than all my other years put together.

1. **One minus two isn't just zero.** The importance of costs and budgeting and basic accounting — stuff I'd never studied in college — stuff that Sherman Leavitt tried to teach me — was not an easy lesson. Of course I hired people who had these skills, but my lack of basic business fundamentals prevented my monetizing, my hard work, and the strong marketing instincts that made our restaurant the most popular pizza eatery in the city for a few years.

2. **If you want a team, you have to *lead* a team.** In about our seventh year, Terry Silver, a respected CPA and my accountant at accounting firm Skoda Minoti, told me at our quarterly meeting that we were losing money at some of our restaurants. He recommended that I cut payroll to keep our cash flow in the positive.
"Either lay off your three general managers at those outlets or lower their wages. They're overpaid and way above industry standard."
I refused out of loyalty to my managers, who were working their butts off. I didn't even mention the matter to my executive staff. I was hoping I could improve the cash flow and profitability through additional sales.
The next quarter Silver told me our financial situation was worse. I resisted again.

The next quarter he told me that if I didn't make a pay cut for these people or fire them, I'd have to take less money and eventually less profits for myself. That did it. I chose my family's financial well-being over my managers' and told my GM of five years that she would have to take a 50% cut in her salary or quit. She quit. I felt terrible but it was a lesson learned. I could have faced this long before but to be honest, I always thought my managers were irreplaceable. In fact, we moved forward without this particular person. Everybody, it turns out, is replaceable.

3. **The captain must always remain on the bridge.** Still as important today as it was thirty years ago: *Be there.* No matter how hard I tried — and I treated my staff well — they could not replicate the emotional investment and focus that I brought as the owner. When I operated six different restaurants in six different locations, it was impossible to create an "employee ownership" mentality. I used all the motivational techniques that I had employed successfully as a coach, and it worked with a few employees, but mostly it was simply not a good model. I did create some real ownership opportunities for a few of my key employees, but compared to real business success, that was cold comfort.

*

INTO THE LAND OF
DREAMS

Dean Adler was the CEO of the Lubert Adler Fund LLC. The LAF had 18 billion dollars under management and Dean was and is considered one of the smartest people in American real estate. He graduated top of his class at U. of Penn Wharton Business School and earned a CPA and law degree before becoming the youngest accounting professor in the history of that school. Today he sits on the boards of the Bed Bath and Beyond company and Albertsons Grocery. Yet the man has no airs about him. He dresses casually and, like some lovable mad scientist, seems never to comb his hair. As it happened, Dean Adler was a close friend of mine and he was about to become my mentor.

Sometime in 1999, I got a phone call.
"Mike? That you?"
"Yeah."

"It's Dean."

"Dean. Wow. How are you?"

"Great, Mike. Mike, listen. I need 1,254 large all-dressed. I need them by Thursday. Can you do it?"

"Dean. Jeez. One thousand and ... what?"

"By Thursday. Noon."

"Well, we could try, Dean."

There was a hearty laugh from the other end.

"I bet you would too," Dean said. A pause, then, "Ever get tired of the pizza business, Mike?"

I was totally off-guard. "Actually, yeah, I do. Sometimes."

"What would you think about a serious business like real estate?"

"What do you mean?"

"I mean we're partnering up with the Florida developer Bobby Ginn. You must've heard of Bobby, Mike. He's practically a legend here. We're going to create a new residential resort in Palm Coast, Florida. You're a smart guy, Mike, and you'd make a natural sales director. Plus you've slung enough mozzarella for one lifetime. Come down and work for Bobby and me."

I was stunned.

"Dean. This is amazing. Really. But there's two problems. First, I don't know anything about real estate. Second, I never heard of Palm Coast."

Dean chuckled. "Don't worry. We'll fix that."

I flew to Jacksonville and from there found my way to Palm Coast, a town just north of Daytona Beach. There I met Bobby Ginn, a likeable, even charismatic man of maybe fifty who was rapidly becoming legendary in the development business. He showed me around the empty site and pointed out where everything was to be built: the condos, the golf course, the tennis courts, beach clubs and fitness centers. I was utterly out of my depth of course and astonished that this busy man would devote so much time to someone he didn't know. Only later did it dawn on me that my friendship with his capital partner might have played a part.

I was tremendously excited at the prospect of starting a new career. Maybe I had seen my last pepperoni with extra cheese. I flew home to Cleveland and almost ran up the sidewalk in my eagerness to tell Sindi and the boys.

Bear with me while I digress briefly to fill you in on my family. We raised our four sons — Ryan, Kevin, Adam and Jonathan — in Pepper Pike, an upper-middle-class suburb of Cleveland. Like all parents, we tried hard to provide an economic quality of life that was an advancement on our own childhoods. Our sons loved our life and had tons of friends and never would have dreamed of moving out of our neighborhood. I believe there's a Midwest/Cleveland thing, an authenticity and down-to-earth way of life compared to many parts of the country.

Sindi, my wife has been as loving a mother and wife as a man could ever have hoped for — a homebody who was nonetheless comfortable with change. Her life centered around raising our boys and she did an amazing job. She was always super supportive of my ideas and jobs and aspirations, and took many chances with me during our early years of marriage. My coaching jobs paid miserably but she was working with mentally challenged adults and earning more than I was. She helped me pay back my graduate college loans and her father helped us buy our first house because I didn't have the money for the down payment.

So this was my family. When I made the decision to work for the Ginn Company in Florida, I had to convince them that this would be a great new opportunity for everyone. I was used to doing fund-raising seminars for my restaurants so I figured I'd do a "family" seminar to persuade everyone to get excited about moving to Palm Coast or St Augustine or Daytona or Jacksonville. I was at my best, reminding them of the year-round sun and warm temperatures, the proximity to Disney World, my chance to earn three or four times more money than I had been earning, the opportunity to meet new friends. This wasn't a move, I pitched them, this was an adventure. I sat back, knowing I'd done a great job. Everyone else spoke their opinion and we took a blind vote. The results were 5 to 1 for *not* moving. I was the only one in favor of the move.

Two days later Bobby made me a formal offer and I had to turn him down. Dean was on the call.

"Hoo boy," he said. "A guy's gotta love his family to take a pass on this one."

Four months later, they were back to me by phone again. Incredibly, it was another job offer.

"We have this thing called a priority selection launch," Bobby told me. "We used it at Hammock Beach and in one afternoon we did $57 million in transactions. So we're moving right on to Orlando. We've acquired the Reunion Resort and Club. It's going to be bigger than Hammock — a lot bigger. But meanwhile, we still need you in Palm Coast."

"I'm sorry, Bobby." I felt like crying. "I'd love to but the family just won't move to Florida. They seem to love the cold."

"No problem!" Bobby laughed. "We're going to get you involved and let you live in Ohio. We're going to create an off-site office with you in charge. You're gonna scrape ice off your windshield *and* make money!"

So I donned the title of Director of Midwest Sales and Marketing for the Ginn Company, conducting seminars across the Midwest and Northeast. I was to spend most of my time recruiting interested second-home buyers and investors and enthusing them about our residential resort opportunity in north-east Florida.

I started the last week of December 1999, commuting to the Hammock Beach site to understand what we were selling, and what sales techniques our team were implementing with our prospects. Bobby contracted RMA, the top sales and marketing group from Atlanta, which was led by a charming demon of a salesperson named Jeff Davis. Jeff took a liking to me and spent a lot of time training me on the psychology of the sale as it applied to the resort residential world. He'd been selling and managing sales teams for the previous 18 years and he looked at this deal as a career move for himself and his team. We went on a five-day retreat to learn the fundamentals of something Jeff Davis called "launch marketing." Launch marketing was a suite of sales strategies employed by this team that were perfect for where we stood in the real estate cycle (and it is a cycle). This was the year 2000, and the banks would lend you as much money as you needed provided you had a pulse. They were even offering "no-doc loans" whereby a prospective buyer could get a loan without having to show his or her income or credit rating. These lending policies fit hand-in-glove with our "second-home resort residential" real estate offerings. Along with the launch marketing strategies such as our "priority selection" events, these lending policies were to help the Ginn companies sell 3.2 billion dollars of pre-construction home sites, condos, and homes. And my seminars and presentations around the

U.S. and Canada would play their part in getting people excited about "fulfilling their dream" — that is, having a second place in Florida.

There were in fact compelling reasons for this excitement. The winter weather in Florida was sunny and warm. There were no state income taxes for full-time Florida residents. The state had enacted a so-called Homestead Act, which protected homes from creditors in the event of the owners experiencing financial hardship. (Remember, real estate follows a cycle, though we didn't normally mention that.) Meanwhile, these owners could live and play with like-minded baby boomers who'd bought the properties around them, everyone living blissfully in world-class golf-course communities with world-class amenities on the beach! And finally and most importantly, those with the luck or perspicacity to buy early would have a home site or home/condo that was appreciating at 10% to 15% yearly. So if buyers didn't like the lifestyle or changed their minds, our sales team had a strong probability of reselling their asset for a profit. Of course we were careful not to promise investment returns, but the subject was never far from anybody's mind.

In the months that followed, I traveled throughout my region putting on Hammock Beach seminars that would excite people about the purchase — not a property, but a 100% refundable reservation to attend our "Condo Launch" at Hammock Beach in June of 2000. From my off-site office in Cleveland, I spent all day on the phone following up with prospects to persuade them to attend one of my seminars or fill out a reservation form. It was a powerful lesson in sales. The phone never rang unless it was my wife asking me when I was coming home, or the sales managers in Florida asking me how many reservations I'd secured that day. All the hundreds of calls each week to strangers, leads, and friends were outbound, generated by me alone. It was tough.

What was I actually selling?

Launch Marketing

Launch marketing is a carefully organized promotional process leading up to what Ginn and his people called the "priority selection event" — and a large-scale closing of sales. Here's how it worked.

I and the entire sales team spent months selling these 100% refundable "reservation certificates" to the priority selection event. A reservation certificate was the only way a potential buyer could attend the event, and the event was the buyer's chance to get in on the ground floor (a figure of speech — these were high-rise buildings) of an opportunity to purchase a home site or condo at this exciting resort residential development. The early reservation holders would have the first choice of the best home sites — best view, best price, best sun exposure, closest proximity to amenities, even a chance of facing the golf course, and other perceived reasons why one site or unit might be better than another. And while we were selling reservation certificates — "certs" we called them — we also offered discounts and privileges through membership in the Founders' Club.

A secret behind launch marketing was the creation in our sales prospects of a sense of urgency and scarcity in respect to these reservations. We relied on the law of averages, by which a certain percentage of the reservation holders would attend the launch event and a certain percentage of these attendees would purchase properties. Provided we sold enough reservations, our success was by this law inevitable and for that reason, the certs were our life blood. We were far more focused on the reservations than the product.

Meanwhile the launch marketing program was supported by an expensive and professional marketing strategy we termed a "drip campaign." The drip campaign kept reservation holders engaged without revealing too much. We would never tell prospects, for example, where they stood in the selection pecking order, nor were they privy to the initial pricing that would be available to Founders' Club members. We fed them just enough to build momentum and excitement, with the promise that, prior to the big launch, they'd have all the information they'd need to make an informed decision.

As the weekend of the selection event drew close, every attendee received a selection book and program. There was real excitement as people arrived from all around the world. We were actually creating a — yes! — a buying frenzy, the ultimate sales tool. Our prospects were transformed into a potent sales force, they were "following the crowd" and possessed by "the power of the many."

The "priority selection event" was modelled on what we knew of Hollywood's style. We provided a lavish cocktail party on the Friday evening, celebrities in attendance, a video that previewed the actual development and finally the presentation of the itinerary for the following day, when our guests would have just 45 minutes to preview their selected unit and make a "buying decision." This was followed by an exclusive Saturday-night dinner party celebrating the community and its newest residents.

Our first launch event was held in December, 2000. Over that one weekend, we sold $57 million worth of pre-construction condos. I made more money in commissions that day than I'd made during the previous two years.

I'm forced now to digress briefly. My topic is the bully.

The Ginn Company was my first serious encounter with the bully. The head office of the company — which I visited regularly — was the stalking ground of a pride of young, aggressive alpha males confined in a highly competitive and lucrative environment. As it happened, most of these males were from the South and ostentatiously proud of their hunting and their fishing — I did neither — and their God. Out in front of these guys was a V.P. of sales — Al by name — who was unfortunately 5'6". (I say unfortunately because his height may have been the root cause of a Napoleon complex.) Al never tired of bragging and it was only a matter of time before my top sales record drew his attention and he demonstrated as much talent for criticizing me as he had for bragging about his sports talent. Because Al, as it turned out, was a classic "jock sniffer" who had never played competitive sports but believed himself to be born to the role and destined to coach. Meanwhile, he worked hard to make me miserable and actually came up to Cleveland to botch presentations in my home town. Finally he resigned to pursue his dream as the coach of a winless sixth-grade girls team at a Catholic middle school in small town South Carolina. This wasn't as bad as being exiled to St Helena like the real Napoleon but it was about right for Al.

Back to The Ginn Company. When I joined in 2000, I was the twenty-third employee. Over the next four years, we used Launch Marketing and its "priority selection" strategies to develop eight more sites in Orlando, Montverde, Florida, Naples, Port St Lucie, Hutchinson Island, Boone, N.C. and St Thomas on Grand Bahama Island. During that period we added another 3000 employees, and sold over $3 billion in real estate. In 2004, after a year of preparation and marketing, we sold in one weekend $470 million worth of pre-construction condos at Reunion Resort and Club in Orlando, Florida. In that state, this remains a record for a single day of sales transactions. I had personally risen to an executive position within the company and was earning a seven-figure annual income.

Then I quit.

I Learn While I Burn: Lesson 3

Errors of Omission

How can someone talk about mistakes after this sort of success? Allow me to explain.

Of all things, success is relative. It's relative to other people's achievements and it's relative to our own expectations. Certainly I wanted to make money, but this ambition masked a deeper ambition: I wanted to run my own show — for the excitement of it, for the sense of fulfilment. Why otherwise had I stuck it out so long at the helm of Captain Tony's?

The Ginn Company experience was exhilarating and a valuable learning experience but it was Bobby Ginn's baby, not mine.

A key point is that, while I was part of The Ginn Company, I was an "all in" player with unlimited commitment and enthusiasm. Certainly this stimulated my performance and that performance was well rewarded. But it also had the effect of blinding me to my deeper aspirations. Why, for instance, didn't I invest more in the very properties I was selling rather than simply work for fees? If I knew so damn much about these opportunities — and I did — why didn't I try harder to build my own wealth by leveraging with debt, and exploiting the refinancing rules? To rub salt in the wounds of these reflections, the few properties I did buy with friends and family did very well.

As part of the same syndrome, the total commitment that made me so effective also blinded me to the inconsistencies in the product we were offering. We rarely mentioned the hidden costs such as neighborhood association fees. And our underlying implication was that every property would appreciate and could always be sold for a profit. This was simply not true. Sure, from 2000 to 2005 the real estate market appreciated in value about 10% yearly and sometime higher. But when the recession hit in 2007, some of the properties that we sold to clients lost 80% of their value. So what? you might reasonably ask. This didn't affect my earnings. But it did affect my personal pride and sense of integrity. Remember, I believed in my product.

And still on the subject of commitment, I also believed in our management and unquestioningly trusted all the intentions of my superiors. Of course I was aware that some of the head guys at The Ginn Company — including our hero Bobby Ginn — were spending money foolishly. I was aware that some of his ideas were downright foolish and delusional. But I was slow to realize that this brilliant guy was only human.

Bobby was a true visionary. With the help of Dean Adler's company, Lubert Adler, he developed over $2 billion of real estate in Florida, North and South Carolina, Colorado, St Thomas, and had a unique way of leading his company. For example, he kept the sales people and the accounting people in separate buildings and tried to prevent them from interacting. In hindsight, it was pure genius. The sales teams tended to reckless behavior and the prima donnas were making three or four times what the nine-to-five accountants made. Ginn knew how to forestall the inevitable jealously and animosity.

Sadly, despite his great success, Bobby had some quirky business traits, most importantly a problem with over-spending. He's never run a pizza eatery and hadn't learned to tie costs to returns. We had five planes and sometimes we'd fly 40 miles from one of our locations to another. We sponsored golf tournaments at Pebble Beach and Hilton Head SC that cost nearly $1 million. The capital partners would keep asking why we were spending so much money.

"Because we'll get a ten-times return from this," Bobby would bark out. "PR and branding, gentlemen! PR and branding!"

Earlier in his real estate career, he'd owned almost 75% of Hilton Head Island, but during the 1980s saving-and-loan crisis, he'd lost it all and the bankers who'd backed him got in huge legal trouble. There were 10,000 bumper stickers driving around that said, "IF GINN OWES YOU MONEY, HONK YOUR HORN." The tragedy of it was that Bobby was exceptionally talented and his passion and work ethic was strong. But along with his other little foibles, he was a deal junkie. At the beginning of the recession in 2006, he decided to invest all of his money (about $40 million) in a NASCAR team called Ginn Racing. He sponsored a few drivers and in 2008, his driver came in second place by two seconds at the Daytona 500. But the difference between first and second place in racing is huge and the next year, Ginn Racing went bust. After creating and managing the most successful resort residential sales organization in the history of Florida, he was nearly broke. Today, Bobby Ginn is living on his farm in South Carolina. He has dabbled in real estate deals but has not been active as a developer for several years. Seems a shame.

Coming back to Michael Friedman, my lack of confidence and my failure to trust my own business instincts — a lot of which probably flowed from my decision to be an employee — were my shortcomings. And while I'm at it, I should mention greed — my greed — that kept me from saying something or trying to change some policy or strategy.

Lastly, there was an omission stemming from ignorance and timidity.

The internet was just beginning to hit the mainstream real estate world. Unfortunately I was not ready to learn it, or embrace the huge advantage of this new communication technology. No excuses: I could have taken classes and worked with people who were at the cutting edge. I snoozed instead on my little pile of cash.

*

ESCAPE FROM LIBERTY HARBOR

My Personal Launch

You, my reader, can appreciate by now that I didn't work my tail off at The Ginn Company for the money alone, as good as that money turned out to be. Whatever else it was, the whole experience constituted an intense training and the professor, whatever his shortcomings, was possessed of a genius I was determined to learn from. In 2005, when I bid farewell to my teachers and classmates at Ginn, I went straight from graduate student to practitioner as the founder of the MF Management Fund.

Stumble at the Block

My plan — this will sound familiar — was to raise funds and invest in "resort residential" real estate. To comply with the U.S.

Securities and Exchange Commission's rules, I was required to use a private placement memorandum (PPM), a legal instrument that assures that all investors are accredited and all risks spelled out. In six months I raised $5 million dollars from 51 private investors. My plan was to invest the $5 million in unentitled resort residential properties that were still at an early stage, then wait for the developer to make improvements, thus increasing the value of these home sites. I would then sell our holdings for a profit. Before I go any further, I want you to admit that it sounds like a good, reality-based business plan.

No doubt you're looking forward to the sad tale of an unwinding deal and then my confessing my sadder-but-wiser mistakes. You sadist, reader.

First, I simply didn't appreciate the immense accounting tasks associated with managing such a fund. Accounting costs money and consumes time. I had a limited amount of both.

Second, based on so little experience with the long-term market, I had no idea of the importance of timing in the real estate investment space. When I started late in 2005, we were just coming to the end of one of the largest real estate bubbles in U.S. history. All my assumptions were predicated on the markets continuing to appreciate at boom levels. So I rushed in, blundered like a blind fool and cost my trusting investors most of five million bucks.

No I didn't. Did you see that coming? I hesitated instead, started getting nervous in 2006 just as I was ready to deploy my first investments. For the first time in six years, properties were not rising in value. In fact, the banks were starting to tighten their debt lending, which, if it went on, would deprive me of the debt leverage I was counting on. But it was too late now. I'd gone too far, had too much momentum. I'd look a fool. I had to invest now, before it was too late.

No I didn't. Instead, I made one of the best decisions of my business career. I closed the fund, admitted my miscalculation, and returned all the monies to my investors with 8% interest. This interest, along with my marketing, accounting and legal fees, cost me about $70,000, by far the best $70,000 I ever lost.

Reinforcements

For a few days, I just sat panting with relief. Then I got a call.

"Michael?"

Steve Wineburg had been one of my investors. He was a short, well dressed guy with a trim build and a distinct Boston accent. He spoke a mile a minute and it was hard to get a word in, which of course made him a terrible listener too. For fifteen years he's prospered in the steel door business.

"Mike, look, what are you doing?"

"When?"

"Today. Or tomorrow."

"Why?" I think I laughed. "What have you got in mind?"

I checked my conscience but it was clear.

"Lunch. I want to take you for lunch."

"That's really nice, Steve. Really. Thank you."

"Mike. I trusted you to invest 350,000 bucks. You saw problems in the market. You gave me my money back with actual interest. Know how many guys'll do that? I want to take you for lunch."

It wasn't lunch. It was a no-bull business meeting that ended in our agreeing to start a new development company. I'd be a 20% equity partner. My role would be to find a property, teach Steve all I knew about Launch marketing, and help develop a resort residential deal.

Meanwhile, Scott Berkowitz dropped by my office. I'd taught him basketball when he was six years old and he was now in the family funeral business. Berkowitz Kumin had a sort of a monopoly in Cleveland's East Side Jewish community but Scott told me he was burnt out with the burial business and had started doing some property title work on his own.

"Mike," he asked me suddenly. "Do you think we could work together in the development business?"

I looked at the young man across the desk, who came off in my eyes like a rich country club kid. On the other hand, he was likeable and, going into this new project with Steve, I could use some support.

"Enjoy working your butt off?" I asked with a smile that probably looked doubtful.

As it turned out, Scott Berkowitz was everything I thought he wouldn't be. He had a strong work ethic and an intensity that matched my own. Our skills were complementary: what I didn't do well, he did. Right off, he found an obscure broker in Tampa who led us to Brunswick, Georgia. Brunswick is one of the small cities on the so-called Golden Isles, a group of barrier islands along the coast. Brunswick is linked to the Georgia mainland by the Sidney Lanier, a tall suspension bridge across a wide body of tidal water now called Fancy Bluff Creek, previously the less romantic Brunswick River. Under the bridge were a hundred-acres of unentitled dirt and a disused paper mill. It was for sale. Here was Steve's opportunity — and ours.

We negotiated a "seller carry" paper. Employing nothing but vision, capital and marketing power, we decided to make this one of the premier river development in Georgia. With our hats set at a jaunty angle, we were off to the races.

I hired the best resort residential marketing company in the country — Epiphany, from Denver — and organized a three-day intensive brain-storming session with architects, the mayor and city officials, an artist, and of course our internal sales team. At the end of the three days we had a mission statement, the outline of a business plan and a name. We called it Liberty Harbor.

We came up with the idea of organizing a "broker's summit" to jump start the reservation process for our "priority selection process." If that sounds vaguely familiar to you, bear in mind that there's only room for so many geniuses in one book and that, if Michael Friedman steals an idea, he only steals from the best. We created an application that real estate agents and brokers had to fill out to even be considered as attendees. The criteria were that they had to have sold or listed over $10 million in the year prior and had to have worked with investors in the past. Of course we'd fly the top brokers in on the Liberty Harbor private jet.

"Private jet?" you say. As it turns out, Steve's rental business owned a few private jets, so we converted one for Liberty Harbor, painted our freshly-minted logo on the tail and had all the seats and napkins and silverware branded with the company name. We held the broker summit at the Jekyll Island Hotel on the nearby island of that name. Over 150 brokers attended the three-hour marathon. The Brunswick city officials were there too, and Steve as our developer. I introduced our sales team — I'd just hired them — and we showed a short video

and some nice artist's renderings of things to come. As you'll understand already, our goal was to get everybody excited and motivated to start securing reservations for our priority selection event four months hence. Those brokers who stayed the night were treated to a boat tour the next morning on the river and a fancy Southern brunch.

Now it was time to go to work.

In all, we staged thirteen seminars in Florida, Georgia, Iowa and North Carolina over the 2006 season. We set up a remote Launch site in Sarasota, Florida and built a sales center at the site in Brunswick. By the end of our campaign we'd accumulated over 950 reservations to attend the priority selection event and claim the right to a priority selection of either a home site or a condo.

By now you know how priority selection events work. I only need to tell you that we sold that day $42 million worth of home sites and

$106 million worth of condos. Local and national newspapers reported this as the second-highest one-day volume of sales transactions in the history of Georgia real estate.

Scott and I, our managers, our sales teams, our outside brokers — we'd knocked it out of the park and we were ecstatic. Steve not so much. He owed us commissions per our agreement but these commissions weren't immediately forthcoming. I was starting to get a bit concerned. Could he access the capital to build what we'd sold? Yet whether he did or no, the man was undoubtedly a visionary and like any visionary he kept pushing on. He began exaggerating our sales to the press by suggesting the we'd sold $400 million worth of real estate, which implied that we'd sold a home on every lot that we did sell. That would be an ambitious goal and could happen some day, but I worried. Wasn't this false marketing?

Now, with Steve in the lead, we planned a follow-up event. We called it a "friends and family appreciation" launch, to be held at the property. We invited our new buyers back to the property for a weekend party, with new home sites and condos to be released to only their friends and family. We offered them a premium — a nice gift and a discounted sales price and free condo dues for a years — for any of their referrals who purchased at this new event. We set up a tent, hired a guitarist and two helicopters, organized kids games and showed a kick-ass video on Friday evening to start the Launch weekend. When it was over, we'd sold another $29 million worth of pre-construction condos and home sites.

So. We'd sold them. Now, we had to, er, *build* them, right? But our lenders didn't look very strong, and our developer had never constructed anything bigger than a bird house — no, wait a minute. He's never actually constructed a bird house. Yet he intended to create a billion-dollar development in some place called Brunswick, Georgia. There was some tension. There were some arguments.

Then something wonderful happened. Centex Homes, a publicly-held home builder, was trying to break into the resort business and they loved what we were doing at Liberty Harbor. Centex people met me at the site and after spending days with Steve and me and our staff, they submitted a LOI to buy our development for $112 million. After sales costs and taxes I'd walk away with about $14.5 million. *This would change my life.*

Steve said no: we'd build what we'd sold. He had an appraisal from a reputable appraisal company for future sale revenues of about $425 million dollars. My mentor and close friend Dean Adler, CEO of the Lubert Adler Fund and massively experienced, called Steve and implored him to sell. He explained — politely, sure — that Steve's obsession with the high appraisal was nuts.

"Sell, man!" he urged. "Sell and walk away with seventy million profit! Live for another challenge! Reinvest with house money!"

"Thanks, Dean," Steve chuckled. "Thanks a lot. But I'm not leaving four hundred million on the table."

I was sick.

Later that year, Steve and I were driving from Jacksonville to the Liberty site and Steve asked me if I would mind taking the wheel. He had a very important call and sure enough, he did. For the next 45 minutes he was engaged in deep speaker-phone conversation with a fortune teller in California. What was happening? Was he having me on? Did he have cancer and this was a last, desperate hope? No, they were talking about *our development* and Steve was *taking notes!*

Finally the call ended. he sat for a while in thought.

"Fantastic woman," he finally said. "Nails it every time."

I kept my hands on the wheel. Steve nodded to himself.

"Far as I'm concerned, she's a gift at $400.00 an hour. I've been using her for years."

We stopped at a gas station and I slipped off to use my phone. Scott answered.

"Scott," I whispered. I looked back over my shoulder. "I'm with Steve somewhere in Georgia. He's been on the phone to a fortune teller for miles!"

"Oh yeah?" Scott snorted a laugh. "What's he gonna do, meet a tall dark stranger?"

"Scott, they're not talking romance. They're talking development strategies!"

"What do you mean? Development of what?"

"*Our* development. This fortune teller in California is the mastermind behind *our development*. Steve takes notes on everything she says."

There was a silence on the other end. I heard him exhale.

"Bullshit," he finally said.

"Scott, listen to me. Steve — our visionary guy, right? — our *guy* — Steve is a *whack job!*"

There was another silence.

"Who's driving?" Scott asked.

"I am."

"Change places, Mike. Get some sleep."

We were still owed our fees, but Steve was focused on the appraisal and the loans it could back. He was pushing his family members to buy the remaining home sites to complete Phase 1. Then suddenly he determined that Scott wasn't all that valuable. He wanted to cut the man's pay. Not surprisingly, Scott decided to leave. I saw the handwriting on the (unbuilt) wall. I negotiated an agreement to sell my 20% for a pay-out over one year. After two arduous but successful years, Liberty Harbor was over for Scott and over for me.

Steve managed the development for three more years. He never succeeded in actually building anything and to this day the home site owners are in possession of their barren pieces of land. Numerous lawsuits were filed and Steve declared bankruptcy. My team was not paid and I lost some of my most valuable capital — the human capital of reputation and relationships.

I Learn While I Burn: Lesson 4

Ignorance is No Excuse

A nice little crop of blunders here.

1. I had no idea at the time the scale of the development we proposed. I concerned myself only with the sales and marketing.

2. I didn't understand that we needed a seasoned developer who was also capitalized. Duh.

3. We had a good marketing program that helped us sell lots of condos and home sites, but the location of Liberty Harbor — Brunswick, the worst location of the Golden isles — would be a long term issue. There was a paper mill on the property during both of our launches. We'd committed to relocate the paper company but had no clue about how to get rid of it. (To the best of my knowledge, the mill is still on the property 13 years later.)

4. At least one of us failed to appreciate how developers need to be transparent with their clients and the media. Exaggeration and promises that a company can't keep are a bad way to build a business.

*

5

TAKING THE HEAT IN
MONTESORO

The Feel of the Wheel

It was 2006 and the great steel wheel of the business cycle was rolling towards us. Not many of us noticed.

A developer named Greg Perlman had purchased 3200 acres in Borrego Springs, California for $18 million. He'd named it Montesoro and envisaged building home sites on the property. Meanwhile a consultant had convinced him to tear up the existing golf course and build a new Tom Fazio signature course. Perlman was a smart businessman, but his expertise was in the area of "affordable" properties, not resort residential properties. The golf course cost $24 million and took three years to finish but as this process neared completion he was getting no traction in his sales process.

A mutual acquaintance told Greg about my expertise in selling home sites and homes in these types of developments. Scott and I invited him to our second friends-and-family launch and he flew into Brunswick with his brother-in-law David.

Greg, CEO and developer of Montesoro, was a exceptionally well dressed man with something of a polished — almost slick — manner. He and David were blown away by how well coordinated our sales process was and by the number of people who were purchasing properties in what was a new and undeveloped project.

After the event, Greg invited Scott and me to Borrego Springs, California to spend a day checking out his development and golf course, which was by then about 80% complete. We traveled five and a half hours by jet to San Diego, then rented a car and got lost on a wild two-and-a-half hour ride through the Anza-Borrego mountain range. When we finally arrived, David greeted us with a warm hug and told us how excited he was to have us at Montesoro.

The place was in the middle of nowhere and a hot dry desert wind was in full force. We made our way to the small but attractive clubhouse. It overlooked the golf course that stood in magnificently lush and green contrast to the desert and mountains around.

Greg was the founder of GH Capital and obviously a financially successful man who wasn't shy about letting us know it. After the initial pleasantries, he put on his sales hat to take Scott and me on a two-hour tour of Montesoro. We looked out at the desert from the air-conditioned coolness of the SUV.

"This is my baby," said our host. "She's mine and I'm passionate about her. Make no mistake about that, guys."

We had an early dinner and then launched into a discussion about how Scott and I and our sales group might work exclusively with Montesoro. It was going to be an exciting challenge, I pointed out. We'd have to, ahem, commute from Cleveland to California almost every week. This didn't appear to faze Greg and in the end we shook hands.

Late that night, the dark drive along crazy mountain roads was scary but we were also excited. This looked like the break we needed.

We stopped in San Diego, where my old friend and mentor, Dean Adler, was at a health spa. Dean listened while we extolled the virtues of Greg Perlman's oasis. When we were done Dean scratched slowly at his mop of hair.

"What year is this?" he asked.

Scott and I glanced at one another.

"2006." I said.

Dean nodded.

"Yeah," he said. "Right. So how do you boys see the business cycle right now? I mean, how do you see the country's appetite for high-end resort residential?"

"Um." Scott looked at me. "Pretty good, I guess. Sure has been."

"Well, you know, Dean," I rushed in. "When the going gets tough …"

"Yeah," Dean sighed. "Right. Look, guys. I love your passion, you know that. But I'm afraid you're out of your minds. Our fund has stopped investing in any second home developments. Think about that. And while you're thinking, think about this: We're not talking Palm Desert here." He took a breath. "We're talking fricken Borrego Springs, men."

We drove to our hotel and flew home to Cleveland the next morning.

Though Scott had left Liberty Harbor by now, I was technically still working for Steve. Dean's words were niggling at me but overall Scott and I were both impressed by Greg's passionate vision. It would be a tough decision. We talked it over at length. There were a few more meetings. Finally agreements were signed and Destination Sales and Marketing LLC was formed. Greg Perlman would be the owner and we would be managing members.

We hired a few of the top sales guys from Liberty Harbor and a few from earlier Ginn developments. I sold them hard on a once-in-a-lifetime opportunity to be a part of golf course development in the desert of southern California. We had houses for them, and we leased three Range Rovers — one for Scott, one for me, and one to be kept on site for any of the sales team that needed it.

We hit the road running, hiring administrative staff and an assistant for Scott, who'd be handling the closing paperwork and compliance with the brokers. After three days, the young woman who'd come in with our top sales agent quit on account of the weather, as she said. The summer temperatures were around 115 degrees. Fall and winter would be windy. But we pushed through every obstacle. Greg was for the most part generous and listened patiently to our sales strategies.

A "charrette" is a French word for a brainstorming session. In our case the objective was to gather information and ideas that would help in the development of our branding and marketing. We invited some twenty-five people from the area to attend our first charrette in order to position our brand and strategies and get all the Montesoro team members to buy into our concept. I was the moderator and the meeting was attended by Greg and his partner and brother-in-law David, by three local architects, by our four new sales people, by a few capital guys and by representatives from Epiphany, our sales and marketing partners. The session went well and a lot of creative ideas were generated. We decided to stage a launch, with the goal of a hundred reservations, with thirty home sites and ten home site/home packages sold.

I hired a total sales team of six, with two assistants. Everybody lived at the development site. We worked six or seven days a week. Scott and I commuted from Ohio every Monday morning and came home on either Thursday or Friday. I'd wake up on Monday mornings, make lunches for my four boys and be picked up at 6:15 a.m. My flight left Cleveland Hopkins at 8:15 and I'd arrive in Los Angeles at 10:35 Pacific time after a five-hour flight. I'd catch a taxi for a forty-five minute ride to the 405 and Sunset in Bellaire, where I'd meet Greg Perlman at his hotel, by which I mean a Holiday Inn he'd bought and rebranded as a hip hotel he called the Angeleno. We'd do a lunch and then I'd make the three-hour drive in our Range Rover to Borrego Springs, though sometimes it was four or five hours. As soon as I'd come through the door of the sales pit — that's what we called our little space at the back of the clubhouse — I'd conduct our Monday afternoon sales meeting, then work until early evening, then collapse into bed around 10:00 p.m. Pacific, which was 1:00 a.m. back home in Cleveland.

We worked with new and old data bases and with direct mail to set up seminars that I coordinated in California at Palm Desert, L.A, San Diego, Irvine, and Laguna, then north in Toronto, Chicago, Cleveland, Mississippi and Columbus, Ohio. Everywhere we went, we'd try to fill the room with a minimum of fifty people and sometimes we got over a hundred. Our emphasis was on the development of a "world premier" golf course community targeted at second-home buyers. Epiphany provided us with great marketing materials. Some of our young sales people were beginning to learn about the internet as a marketing tool, especially something people were calling "social media." Our sales room had a charged competitive atmosphere, with Ann, who'd worked with me at Ginn, and David, who'd worked with me at Liberty Harbor, competing for one another's leads. There were some fiery meetings and I had to play judge and jury to ensure nobody got really upset.

We decided to stage our launch event in the summer of 2007 and chose the La Costa Hotel in San Diego because temperatures out in the desert were, as said, often above 115 degrees. Our ploy was to haul in loads of sand, cacti, palm trees and transform the ballroom of the La Costa into a miniature of the Montesoro site. The result was stunning. Four days before the event, we all got together to preview the cut-rate promotional video that Scott had commissioned a local broker to produce. We dimmed the lights as the opening shots came up. Then there was silence. Then some muffled noises.

"Hey!" Young Larry was one of our best sales recruits. "Hey," he said. "This looks like the opening of that porn movie I watched the other night."

"Larry." Sal was his buddy. "Larry, you gotta start watching better quality porn, man."

"Is this it, Scott?" I asked. "Because if it is, we could break the real estate market for years."

"Okay okay," Scott was clearly mortified.

"Scott, we've got four days!"

"Okay, Mike."

"Elva!" I called. Elva was our marketing partner from Epiphany who'd done so much since coming aboard.

"I'm here, Mike."

"Elva, can you save our sorry asses?"

"I can try."

And over the next few days, she did. She didn't sleep for 38 hours, flying from Colorado to San Diego to Las Cruces, New Mexico to work with a video guru who specialized in high-quality editing and effects. She showed up at 5:00 p.m. on the Friday evening before the Saturday launch. Greg Perlman wanted to preview the final result. We nervously loaded the video. He watched it.

"This is spectacular," he said.

After eight months of exhausting effort, the Priority Selection Event for the launch of the Montesoro development was about to happen.

We opened with a cocktail party for our prospective buyers and a lot of final sales positioning and networking. I stood up and spoke, as did Greg. The video was a hit and earned a huge ovation. We sat down for a celebratory dinner with our future home owners, then most of our team went out and partied.

We started work at 6:30 the next morning, setting up booths and the breakfast for our early reservation holders. I stopped by the booth we'd designated for our closings and noticed there were no closing docs. The escrow people from the law firm looked anxious.

"Where's Scott?" I asked. Scott was in charge of closing all the deals and would have the closing docs ready to go for that morning.

Bill, one of our managers, cleared his throat.

"Um, I believe he's hiding from you."

"Hiding? Why?"

"Because he knows you're going to go crazy."

"And why would I do that?"

"Um, I guess he left instructions at the San Diego Kinkos and he … forgot to double check if they were done and they … forgot to do it."

"Oh my God."

"Also Flagstar — that's our go-to lender for our clients, right? — I guess Flagstar has decided they're not going to fund the home sites and lots. I believe all our buyers were depending on that."

A person can only take so much good news at once. We had no choice but to put on a strong front. Scott bribed the La Costa Hotel to make thousands of copies of the closing docs. Flagstar suddenly decided to make some small exceptions and give our clients partial financing. In the end, after a one-hour delay, the launch went off pretty smoothly and we sold $37 million worth of real estate. It was a strong number but we weren't 100 per cent satisfied because we'd been hoping to convert the 100 reservations into some $50 million in sales. As it was, a lot of the buyers were friends and family of Greg and, worse, our expected out-of-town reservation holders didn't attend in the big numbers we'd hoped for.

Greg took us out to a Ruth's Chris Steak House to help celebrate our eight months of hard work and our successful launch. I was personally exhausted and ready to go back to Cleveland for a week or two to see my family but I knew we needed to do some extensive follow-up with our new buyers. They were protected from buyer's remorse by a two-week rescission clause, so we had to keep them engaged and happy during the post-launch period. Nonetheless I let our top three sales people take off for three weeks. It was a huge mistake. We lost 20% of our sales as a result of poor follow-through.

I stayed at the helm for a lonely few weeks, on my own in the sales center, trying to beat out fires in all sorts of development and sales issues. Finally I left Borrego for two weeks at home in Cleveland.

When I returned, Greg and I sat down and discussed the next launch. It was 2008 and we could already see we were in the early/middle stages of a major recession. We could already see that this was a terrible time to be selling high-end secondary homes designed for an expensive private-golf-club lifestyle but located in a remote part of California. We could already see that our current sales strategies just weren't going to work. What to do?

Our golf director and our construction director and I came up with a plan to convert some of our old and new houses to "fractionals." Fractional properties were cousins of time-sharing properties but they entailed actual ownership of a house. It was easier to treat a fractional as you would traditional real estate, with leveraged finance, depreciation, and tax write-offs for interest payments.

Furthermore, fractional real estate was usually a higher-end product in a higher-end resort. It didn't have the negative stigma that the time-sharing industry had earned, where sales people were known to be savage practitioners of hard-core sales tactics. And fractionals seemed to make a lot of sense during a recession, since the wealthy loved to travel, loved to have some sort of second home but now, in increasingly difficult times, loved to pay only for a fraction of the costs — the utilities, the taxes and all the usual burdens associated with home ownership.

I thought back to my days at the helm of Captain Tony's. My lunch clients didn't want to eat an entire pizza, but they loved buying one or two slices. As the owner, I could and did charge a premium for the slice, since it's a value for people not to have to buy an entire pizza. Same principal.

I spent the next months traveling to different fractional communities and Scott and I attended a few fractional/time-sharing conferences in San Francisco and Palm Desert. We quickly became experts and I hired a sales consultant from Canada to help us with our next launch. We had to organize a complete new boot camp and retrain our sales team to understand the concept of fractional real estate. Scott started working with Greenberg Traug, a speciality law firm from Miami, Dallas and L.A., to learn the legal side and understand the documentation we needed to be able to sell these "fractions."

Greg was not convinced that this strategy would work but I pushed him hard to let us try a program. It was expensive — yes, and risky — but as the recession crept in, we were going to have a tough time following up on our first launch. It was hard to avoid the sense that people were not looking to buy second houses while their stocks and savings were in free fall and financial institutions were going bankrupt. But who had a better idea?

We spent the next three months securing reservations for our second launch — the fractional home launch. By now I don't need to describe how we went about it and how hard we worked. You know.

The launch was scheduled for March 2008 at Montesoro. Greg had been patient until we'd lost 20% of our buyers through delays in follow-up. Now he became noticeably less responsive to me and when he was responsive, he was real edgy.

"What's Scott up to?" he asked one day. "I mean, really? I mean, what's his role? There's no more launch sales to close, right?"

I got it. For the first time, I started feeling nervous about our future.

And finally — the second launch was launched. And it was … a bust! — my first real failure in an eight-year sales career. We sold five fractions and three home sites. The next day, Sunday, March 23rd, Greg told me to let Scott know he was no longer needed.

A few weeks later, my phone rang. It was Aida Turbo, whom I'd met first in Boca Raton in 2003 when I was looking for markets I could sell to for the Ginn Company. She was one of the most powerful real estate brokers in the world and she would help me learn the international real estate world. She worked on the educational side with the National Association of Realtors, teaching people in six languages and across the globe how to conduct real estate transactions. We'd hit it off immediately. In 2004, sponsored by the NAR, we traveled extensively: Brazil, Argentina, St Thomas, the Bahamas and elsewhere. While Aida was teaching classes and seminars, I was meeting the ultra-wealthy who were looking to get some of their money into the U.S.

Now, as darkness seemed to be falling over the Montesoro adventure, she was on the phone.

"Mike," she began. "Would you be interested in speaking to a good friend of mine from Spain, name of Pablo Pinero?"

"Of course," I laughed. "Of course I'm going to speak to any friend of yours, Aida." Did she think I was an idiot?

"Well, Pablo's a really wealthy and successful owner and developer of a group of all-inclusive resorts in Mexico, Spain, Jamaica, and the Dominican Republic. These are all ocean front, Mike, and they feature packaged single-price seven-day holidays. Pablo uses professional promoters and he's printing money, Mike."

"That's great, Aida. Great. So why's he need me?"

"He needs somebody because he's decided to expand his ownership in Akumal, Mexico and he's purchased the land across the street from his existing resort. He intends to build a resort/residential development and he's going to build it around a Robert Trent Jones Signature golf course, with townhouses and condos for sale."

"It has a familiar ring, for sure."

"Look, Mike. They've been trying to sell pre-construction home sites and condos for about a year but so far they're going nowhere, things being what they are. Pablo called me yesterday and asked me if I knew a great marketing team that could help him accelerate sales."

"And you thought of me?"

"I did."

"Even knowing I'm doing Montesoro?"

"I know about Montesoro. How's your Spanish?"

"No speaka."

"Yeah. Well, Pablo don't do the English either. I'll arrange an interpreter."

Our call the next day went on for some 45 minutes and ended with Pablo Pinero inviting me to visit his team in Mexico. I got off the phone and called Scott. He was already back at home with his wife and kids in Cleveland.

"Come on," I pleaded. "It's a sunny paradise on the ocean, man."

"So?"

"Listen, it's two, maybe three hours shorter than the commute to Montesoro. You could be with the family more often."

"Would you do it?"

"If it's any good, sure."

"Hm."

"Come on, Scott. Whatta we got to lose?"

"That's true."

Back at Montesoro and just before the disastrous launch, I'd met Rick Vesci, who worked for an outfit in San Clemente that syndicated 1031 buyers, and I'd invited him to our launch to observe. Two months after the failed launch, Greg and I met and agreed that it was time for somebody else to lead the team. To my surprise, Rick took over as president of sales. I guess he'd had that in mind. Nine months later the Montesoro development went into a downward spiral and Greg let the entire team go. Nine months after that, I learned that Rick and his wife had both been fired and escorted from the property by local police.

I Learn While I Burn: Lesson 5

Nothing Succeeds Like Failure

A lifetime of business venturing has taught me this amazing fact: in any field of endeavor, including sales, the number of things you don't know is unlimited — and so are the opportunities to learn. Here are a few quick lessons from the school of Montesoro.

1. Follow-up is as important as the initial sales efforts. As one of my toughest sales teachers once told me, "Sales mean nothing but closed sales can cure cancer." We worked for eight months with a great plan in a tough market and would have closed many additional sales if our team — and I — had committed to a longer and better follow-up program.

2. Working harder gives you a better chance to succeed but sometimes working harder doesn't work. We labored seven days a week for an average of sixty hours a week. What we generated was burn-out and friction.

3. Timing trumps all. You can have a great product, great marketing, a great cost basis, a great team and great strategies. And you can fail anyway because of market conditions at the time.

*

BLOWING IT
IN BAHIA

I think both Scott and I were happy to be working together again. In the spring of 2007, we flew from Cleveland to Cancun, rented a car at the airport and drove about 30 minutes to Pablo Pinero's resort at Bahia Principe. The style was a pleasing sort of Spanish/Mexican, on the ocean, with several beautiful pools. We were greeted by Pablo's son-in-law Michele, who spoke a fractured but intelligible English. We talked for an hour before he offered us the job.

Over the next few days we negotiated our deal, inspected the development, and checked out the local competitors. The Pineros had several sales people on board already, most of them bilingual or trilingual. They were clearly both excited and apprehensive at the prospect of the REvision Group taking over the sales operations. Meanwhile I wanted to bring in a sales director I could trust and who was comfortable with Mexico and its culture. Chris Dufek had worked with me at the Ginn Company and we'd become friends. He'd since worked in Mexico, Portugal, Costa Rica, Colorado, Florida and Texas. I called him up and made a passionate recruiting pitch for him to become our sales director. I told him about the beauty of this resort with the signature golf course home sites across the street. I emphasized that he'd be able to use all the amenities — the beach, the beach club, the fitness center, all the other recreational features. Chris was just finishing his first year at a pre-construction deal in Portugal and wasn't much interested in moving, but he did love Mexico. I offered him a higher than normal salary and higher than average override on our closed sales. My former time-sharing sales directors and marketing gurus I'd brought in to help were reluctant to include Chris in the new venture. They thought that I could serve as the sales director, with Scott as the marketing and closing executive.

"We're top heavy, Mike," they protested.

I waved this off. I didn't feel I could pull it off without my team, and since this was my deal, I won that argument. I got back to Chris in Portugal and persuaded him to visit. The next week he flew to Cancun.

One of the curious aspects of modern business is the way you can build real relationships over long distances, sometimes without meeting in person. Mutual interest is the glue that binds. I'd spoken to Chris maybe twenty-five times over the five years since the Ginn Company. When we finally met at the resort, we hugged like old friends though I hardly recognized him.

We shared some laughs and war stories, then got down to the serious business of a job interview.

"What the hell is that?" I wanted to know.

He had been lugging this huge contraption that now stood beside him. Why would he bring this thing — whatever it was — across the ocean to Mexico?

Chris stroked the thing fondly.

"You remember Jeff Davis, our old sales mentor at Ginn?"

"Of course."

"Remember him lecturing us on 'precursor faith'? You act like the future will be a certain way and that helps steer the future?"

"Yeah."

"So this is my wind surfing kite and you're going to offer me this job and I'm going to say yes and this will be one less thing I'll have to bring when I move here."

You have to hire a guy like that.

So Chris would manage sales and Scott would work on the fractional sales side and I would manage the entire process and at the same time conduct sales seminars in Canada, Mexico and the U.S. The REvision Group's Bahia assignment was underway.

We would sell both whole ownership and fractional ownership. We conducted a charrette and an intensive three-day boot camp training session for our sales team of 16 people from Italy, France, Spain, Canada, U.S., Russia and of course, Mexico. I myself started doing seminars across the U.S. and Canada the following week. The secret of a successful seminar of this sort is to fill the room with qualified second-home prospects, then deliver a dynamic presentation that gets the participants excited about "test driving" — visiting our property and spending a few days on the ocean with 80 degree temperatures and breathtaking views. When they'd experienced that, we liked to say IFO — It's Fricken Over. Close the deal. Easy peasey. In the bag.

The first few months saw some good leads through direct marketing and open houses at the property. Our brochure went into every hotel room across the street. Some referrals started to come in. I hired a couple from Florida and we started traveling together twice a month to various cities. We did two shows in Houston that the head of the Pinero family came as an observer. There were 125 people in a room that only held 85. We were on a roll.

Our two-tier sales program gave our buyers the option to purchase either whole ownership or a fractional ownership. Couldn't miss.

The only flaw in an otherwise flawless plan is that we weren't making sales. I slowly realized that Chris was getting discouraged and I had constantly to keep him in a positive frame of mind. I couldn't afford to lose this vital cog in our sales and marketing team.

Then the bombshell.

We had our regular sales meeting scheduled on a Tuesday but Scott didn't show up. I was a little surprised. Scott and I both prided ourselves on never being late for a meeting. If we couldn't attend, we always called. After the meeting, I called his cell and he answered. He was clearly out of breath and the connection was bad.

"Scott!" I shouted. "What's going on?"

"Mike?"

"Yeah. Scott, you weren't at the meeting. Where are you?"

"Mike. Sorry. I'm going through international security in Cancun airport."

"What are you saying?"

"Mike, I love you, but this swine flu thing here has me scared. I've had it with the travel for now, Mike."

"But the development."

"I'm sorry, Mike. I'm out. I want to be at home with my wife and two boys. Gotta go, Mike. Sorry as hell."

My group started to feel pressure from the Pinero family. We kept ensuring them that building a pipeline of prospects takes a while. Wait for the big launch event, we said, but upper management decided they did not want to invest in an event unless we produced some traditional sales. We'd sold about four home sites and a few fractionals.

I'd been able to explain Montesoro away but now for the first time in my ten-year sales career, I realized that trying to sell second houses — whole or fractional or whatever — in the middle of a recession was nearly impossible. It was real tough to be selling a "want" when people just had "needs." Yet I couldn't share my insight with my team. I lay awake at nights. The economy counts, stupid!

But it got worse. Also for the first time as a leader of a sales team — or any team for that matter — I realized my team was not acting like one. Office gossip and back-stabbing were starting to appear. I'd always taken pride in creating a team environment, with healthy competition and cooperation. But I seemed to have forgotten that the leader has to be present and everybody has to buy into the mission. The truth was that I was only there eight or ten hours a week. The pressure from the Spanish owners was increasing and the language differences were creating barriers. Chris was a great guy but wasn't cut out to be a strong team leader. I tried to keep everyone motivated, but I was losing them and I had to accept that it was me who'd put this mess together.

The developers from Spain wanted to see what was going on. I coordinated three seminars cum dinner presentations in Denver and they assured me they'd be there. I counted on the Florida couple and a few internal people in Mexico to draw in a large number of attendees such as we'd had in Houston, when we'd signed fly-and-buy deals right at the show. Now we put the usual strategies to work — some local marketing with local brokers and a raft of e-mails to our current Denver database. We also tried a new program: it would cost just $1500 to send out one million texts in the Denver area. I was very excited about this new marketing technique. If we got just 0.001% of the people we'd invite via text, we'd have 100 potential prospects. What could go wrong?

Everything. One of the venues didn't even have a screen to show our PowerPoint show. Our one million texts brought eleven people. Disaster. We cancelled the last show of the three and the owners left early — pissed. I was upset, embarrassed, disappointed with my seminar partners and with the team in Mexico. And with myself.

On the flight from Denver back home to Cleveland, I decided I was going to resign. Astonishingly, when I announced this, the owners were not ready to give up on our team and me. But I knew in my heart that I couldn't reach the sales goals in that economy and with the difficulty of managing my team. I called the owners back and really did resign in the summer of 2007. Chris wanted to quit as well, but he stayed on as a favor to me for another five months. Happily he met a local Mexican girl and they started going out and became a couple. He deserved the consolation.

I Learn While I Burn: Lesson 6

Where and When Should a Leader Be?

From Bahia I learned that there were personal factors that could contribute to failure — and impersonal factors. The successful business person learns to recognize both and draw the most useful conclusions.

1. In real estate, timing is always the trump card, more important than product and sponsor and sales and marketing strategies. Our huge efforts on behalf of the Bahia development were made in the middle of the Great Recession. We did very much what we've done for other developments, but tough timing is sometimes impossible to overcome.

2. I keep "learning" this one over and over through my career: No matter what business — pizza eateries, sales management, real estate development — the leader has to be 100% engaged and present at the front of the action.

3. I lost my control as I brought too many partners. When I depend on outside sources and other people, there's the risk they may not have the work ethic or attitude that I have. Whatever, it doesn't end well for me!

4. Simple human sensitivity is a virtue in and of itself. But insensitivity can have its own practical consequences. I should have been more sensitive to Scott and his young kids and should have given my trusted partner more leeway in respect to his travel and ability to work remotely. Fortunately Scott was wiser than me in this instance and we went on to work together again.

*

MIDNIGHT IN THE
OASIS

The years 1999 to, say, 2006 had been the bad old days for U.S. real estate. Not that anyone noticed. In fact, those years had felt really good at the time. Because large developers could count on the continuous appreciation of property values, they were able to obtain deposits on all or most of their units during the pre-construction phase and this almost guaranteed bank financing. When construction was complete and the price of units jumped, the original buyers could flip their (never occupied) units at significant profit. It was like magic — as long as the market held.

The bubble burst. When Barack Obama inherited the mess in 2008, he described Ft Myers, Florida as "ground zero" for the collapse of the real estate bubble. The city was host to thousands of foreclosures. Bankruptcy auctions were regular events.

In 2009 I founded the REvision Group, whose mission was to help creditors dispose of distressed properties. By 2010 we were struggling to re-market a failed resort development on Ute Lake near Tucumcari, New Mexico. It wasn't going well. Meanwhile I'd met Jon Gollinger, the high-profile founder and CEO of Accelerated Marketing Partners, which specialized in helping developers sell real estate through auction-like events. I started working in Baltimore with Jon, who at the time was selling distressed townhouses and condos in the harbor area.

In the early spring of 2012, I got a call from my friend and real estate mentor, Dean Adler, the CEO of the Lubert Adler Fund LLC (LAF). I've mentioned Dean a few times already. LAF had 18 billion dollars under management and Dean was and is considered one of the smartest people in American real estate. He graduated top of his class at U. of Penn Wharton Business School and earned a CPA and law degree before becoming the youngest accounting professor in the history of that school. Today he sits on the boards of Bed Bath and Beyond and Albertsons Grocery. Yet the man has no airs about him. He dresses casually and, like some lovable mad scientist, seems never to comb his hair.

Dean wanted me to travel to Ft Myers, Florida to check out the Oasis — two condo towers of 220 units each — originally developed by the Related Group out of Miami. But Related had defaulted on a $200 million note and Steven Ross, CEO of Related, was now somewhat cheekily thinking about purchasing the property at a discount from the Bank of America's bankruptcy department.

I booked a flight to Ft Myers the next day and met with some of Dean's due-diligence team and a few local brokers. I was intrigued to learn that Ft Myers was just completing a $40-million re-development aimed at creating a more gentrified downtown. There was a new pedestrian area and all sorts of new clubs and restaurants. I realized that the city was on a nice river and had good access to world-class beaches. The same sun that shone on more successful west-coast cities — Naples, Bonita Springs, Sarasota, Tampa Bay — shone on Ft Myers, which was actually somewhat closer to the East Coast and Midwest. Last but not least, Florida has no state taxes.

I toured the Oasis on my second day in Ft Myers. It was impressively sited on the banks of the Caloosahatchee River, with first class amenities, a great resort pool in each building, large modern fitness centers and stylish lobbies. It was also completely empty. With the economy in shambles the condo units had actually depreciated since their initial offering in 2008 was snapped up by speculators on Related's list, each of which plunked down a 20% deposit. Now, in 2011, the banks were unwilling to finance the investors' remaining 80% of the purchase price of the units, so when the time came to close the sales, everybody bailed. Well, not everybody.

"Hi," I said when a man in his sixties answered the door of unit #203.

"Hi." It seemed like he'd been expecting me. "Can I help you?"

"I think so," I said. "I'm Michael Friedman. Aren't you the guy who was on the Larry King Show, talking about your condo?"

"Yes. That's me."

"Because of the 440 units in the Oasis, you're the only occupant?"

"Correct."

"Why is that?"

"The recession, I guess."

"No no. I mean, why are you here?"

"Me? I'm here because it's a great place to be. Why wouldn't I be?"

"Okay," I said. "Like, you're a total original, then."

He laughed. "No I'm not. I just happen to be the first of the real buyers."

I looked at the man.

"You may be right," I said.

I called Dean and told him what I'd seen and learned. The Oasis was a good property in itself though the location was in a rough part of the downtown. However, the downtown was being redeveloped and could eventually comprise an improving market. Overall, the asset had potential if his group could complete a purchase at a significantly discounted price.

"Thanks, buddy," Dean said. "I really appreciate this. Listen, Mike, it's likely George Perez and the Related people will be interviewing sales teams to help him sell these units."

"Oh yeah?" I could feel my pulse quicken. "If they buy it, right?"

"Well, the note's for $201 million and we're talking about getting it for $49 million."

"I get it."

As soon as I was back in Baltimore I called the Related Group and asked if I could make a presentation to build the sales team for the condos once the new LLC closed the purchase. The guy at Related told me there were four other groups competing for the opportunity to sell these units, but he did agree to accept my request. I had two weeks to put together a dynamite sales and marketing plan.

I was still working with Jon Gollinger. His Accelerated Marketing Partners (AMP), with its focus on urgency and (if done correctly) scarcity, was especially useful during these recessionary times when banks and trustees needed to get properties off their books. I knew AMP would be the perfect group to partner with, but there were two problems: First, Jon was still busy handling those distressed townhouses and condos in the harbor area. Second, the guy was an alpha male, par excellence. I could picture my own — and very new — REvision Group and this, our first really major opportunity, getting totally swamped in his wake.

I flew from Baltimore to Miami and booked a place at The Viceroy, Dean Adler's hotel in South Beach. I looked more deeply into the Oasis property and the real estate opportunity. The Related Group and Lubert could purchase the note for about 26% of the actual value, so I concluded we could sell the units to the public for about 50% of the original price and make a ton of money for the developers, offer great deals to the buyers, and earn strong fees for REvision. My excitement grew by the day. Here was a true win-win-win.

I decided that our Launch marketing programs (which were so successful in Florida with the Ginn Company and in Liberty Harbor) would have to be incorporated. I called the mayor of Pompano Beach, Lamar Fisher, a trusted friend and great guy with a stellar reputation who also happened to be the CEO of the Fisher Auction Company. We agreed to put together a joint venture to sell the Oasis's units via auction and we worked for days on the presentation we'd make to the Related Group.

On a March morning we went to the Related Group's headquarters in South Beach, Miami, and were shown into the office of CEO George Pérez, the legendary South Beach developer. I'm afraid something of George's reputation for taste and arrogance had gone before him and, sure enough, he was wearing a thousand dollar suit and had a million dollars worth of art hung on the walls around him. (Any connection between George and the Pérez Art Museum Miami is no coincidence.) It was said that George, born in Cuba and raised in Argentina, was a tenacious businessman who demanded that his employees act as if they were better than anyone else. They could get away with a certain bullying management style because of their tremendous success in Miami real estate. A book detailing George's rise to billionaire status was actually lying on his desk.

But Lamar and I were determined not to worry about any of

this. We were too pumped and too ready. I took the lead, speaking fast as Lamar ran the slides of our two-hour PowerPoint presentation. My strength is generally in creating a hopeful and optimistic atmosphere and I projected a hundred units sold at our first auction. I spoke for almost two hours and when I was finished, pretty exhausted, the CFO Matt Allen thanked me and said they would get back to us.

The next morning I got a call from Dean.

"Look Mike," he said. "Don't be too disappointed if Related picks a big, better-known group. There's only so much I can do."

But two days later, I got a call.

"Mr Friedman? This is Karen." Karen was Related's director of development and one of Pérez' key employees. "Mr Friedman, you and your REvision Group have been awarded the job. Congratulations."

I was just able to stop my phone from slipping out of my hands.

"I'll tell you, Mr Friedman," Karen went on. "George really loved your enthusiasm and he's confident you and your partner will have the energy and drive to sell out all of one building — 220 units. George is always right about these things."

"Thank you, Karen," I said. "It'll be a cinch."

I hung up and then I actually screamed out loud, though nobody was there to share my jubilation.

This was now June, and we proposed an auction date of mid-November. Lamar and I put together our plan for the next six months. He'd been taught by his father, famous Florida auctioneer Benny Fisher (also a former mayor of Pompano Beach) and had been in the auction business for 40 years. Our promotional tag line was "Never Before and Never Again." Never again would buyers have the opportunity to buy a new condo on the river in Ft Myers for a 50% discount on the original price. Our goal was to bring 250 qualified buyers to the auction in Ft Myers.

There are two types of real estate auction strategies. The "absolute" method promotes sales with no minimum starting price, on the theory that this attracts more participants, creates more excitement, and may drive prices up through a frenzy of eagerly competing bids. You might think of this as true, market-based capitalism, with the accompanying risk that initial bids might be so low that even with competitive bidding, assets might be sold for less than reasonable market value. The "minimum reserve" method, on the other hand, protects the price integrity since the seller will not accept any price lower than the minimum reserve set up prior to the auction. The risk here is that a minimum reserve auction may limit the number of bidders, as the minimum price might keep people from attending. Less competition may mean lower selling prices.

My gut inclination was to be a bit conservative and use the minimum reserve method, but Lamar was adamant that the absolute method would bring a better result. I deferred to his expertise because I'd grown to really like and respect the man. Our joint venture agreement was very fair and I negotiated with Related for a $12,000 monthly draw for the four months leading up to the sale. Yes, I'd had some reservations when I first partnered up with Lamar, since Jon Gollinger from Accelerated Marketing Partners was doing a lot more deals with a higher degree of sophistication. But I wanted more control than I would have had with Jon and I was able to negotiate a better split of fees with Lamar than Jon would have given me.

Now we mined Lamar's database while the Related Group's advertising company took out expensive ads in Florida, New York, and Boston newspapers. For the next four months, I lived in Ft Myers and traveling weekdays to eleven cities across the U.S. and to Toronto, Canada. Our beautiful marketing brochure and strong PowerPoint promoted our seminars as opportunities to purchase a retirement or second home in sunny Florida. Sometimes Lamar would join me and even George Pérez made a token appearance at a few of the seminars.

Meanwhile a small fly began to appear in the ointment. On close examination, the fly turned out to be my old nemesis. What Lamar and I didn't know was that the Related Group's asset management and marketing team was a nest of bullies —mean-spirited and demeaning to everybody, including their own staff, their vendors, their brokers and their new partners, the REvision Group/Fisher Auction. Queen bully was the anal Karen, who wanted to micro-manage every decision Lamar and I made. Unless you think this is special pleading on my own behalf, remember that Lamar had been doing auctions for his entire life, and his father Benny, who founded the Fisher Auction company in the 1960s, had been enshrined in the Auction Hall of Fame. Karen wasn't intimidated. She demanded that she be included in all e-mails sent to our and the Related team. When I conducted a charrette, where it was my sole responsibility to coordinate and lead, she addressed me afterwards.

"I couldn't wait till that session ended, Mike," she said too loudly. "Now it's my turn to be in charge." I thought she was kidding.

Yes, Lamar and I should have demanded complete authority from the start, since we had been hired to be the exclusive sales and marketing team. Yes, I should have told Karen to stop trying to manage our process. But in fact I didn't have the guts. Related was in the driver's seat, the woman was fiercely loyal to George Pérez, and I was worried she might decide to fire us during the pre-auction process. She insisted we hire a very expensive Miami-based marketing company. This was a waste of time and money and precipitated a pointless power struggle between Lamar and I on the one hand and the marketing group on the other. Karen then brought in a national brokerage group from Baltimore. I was opposed to both decisions but it hadn't escaped me that if we were successful with this deal, we could leverage the success to promote the REvision Group across the USA. Better to bite the bullet. Thus is the bully often rewarded?

And in the fourteen weeks before the auction, we crushed it. On a perfect Saturday morning in November, under blue skies, with abundant sunshine and temperatures around 74 degrees, we opened the doors at the Convention Center on the river in downtown Ft Myers. Over 700 attendees flooded in. Of these, some 275 had come with a $10,000 cashier's check qualifying them to bid, and among them, reporters and media people from national and local newspapers and TV interviewed me and Lamar. They all wanted to know how we'd attracted such a strong response in so short a time, with excited people traveling from sixteen states and six countries, all hoping to bid for a discounted condo at Oasis. Suddenly Related Group staff appeared and insisted that no media were allowed. People who'd come from New York and Toronto to write about the event were summarily kicked out.

We'd decided based on Lamar's expertise and experience that the first 40 units would be sold in an absolute auction, and then the remaining 60 units would be sold with a minimum reserve price.

At 10:30 a.m. Lamar opened the bidding. The air was electric. I could feel my heart pounding as three or four bidders competed for the first unit. Lamar brought the gavel down at a price a bit higher than we'd expected. I could barely restrain my excitement. The second unit went up and again a number of bidders drove the price to a gratifying number in excess of $200,000. Lamar was calm. We were going to make a ton of money. The third unit pushed through to an even bigger number. I glanced over at George Pérez and Karen and their Related people. Were they smiling?

The fourth unit came up and bidding started at $100,000. A few paddles went up. I craned my neck in search of the next bidders. One came in. Another. $150,000.

"Alright, folks." Lamar looked around the room. "Let's move along smartly. There's a lot of amazing condos we're going to sell this day."

Silence.

"Alright, folks. Let me see $160,000 then."

Finally a paddle.

"May I see $170,000 then. $170,000."

Nothing. Lamar frowned and several heartbeats later, brought down the gavel.

"Sold for $160,000."

Problem was, the units were all pretty similar. It wasn't like Lamar could move along from silver tea sets to old mahogany dining chairs. With Lot #4 going for a little over $150,000, nobody wanted to pay more than $150,000. A few more lots went by at that level and I could hear angry voices. I looked across the room to where Pérez and his people had been sitting. Several were now standing and glaring at me. I retreated into a side room as they advanced, Pérez at the fore.

"Okay, that's it," he ordered as he came through the door. "That's enough. Stop it now!"

"What?"

"Stop this circus!"

"The auction? We can't stop the auction, George."

"I'm telling you to stop it or else!"

"How can I stop the auction, George?"

Who did he think he was? King Canute? Auctions are governed by law. He stormed back to the main room.

"There'll be consequence for this, Mike," Karen barked over her shoulder as she followed him. You'd never have guessed they'd bought these units new for a quarter of their original price

At the front, Lamar had just sold Lot #29 for $155,000.

"That's it!" Pérez called as he marched up the aisle. "It's over!"

Lamar looked down calmly.

"The next lot is number 30," he said. "Who'll open the bidding?"

"Nobody!" Pérez shouted. "It's over!"

"The first 40 lots are without reserve, as advertised," Lamar said. "Auctions in the state of Florida are governed by the laws of the state of Florida. Who'll open the bidding?"

There was an angry buzz as Pérez huddled with his crew. Lamar proceeded and I realized that bidding was in fact pretty steady up to the $150,000 mark. If we could get through the first 40 lots, there was enough momentum, maybe we'd sell the final 60 at above reserve. But after a second interruption, George stopped the sale when Lot #40 had sold. His lawyers knew his rights. Shocked attendees were told to go home.

"George! Please!" I begged. "We're going to move right along to the minimum reserve phase. Don't stop us now!"

"Get outta here, all of you!" George shouted. "And by the way, both you jerks are fired!"

Immediately, my phone began to ring.

"Michael?" A vaguely familiar and very plaintive voice. "We've come all the way from Minnesota because of you. We haven't even bid yet! Michael, what's going on? Please!"

There were another dozen such calls in the next fifteen minutes. Some folks had come from as far as Europe. In all, 175 qualified buyers were shut out. Ten minutes after Related cancelled the auction, I slipped back to my apartment and sat pondering for an hour. I knew George and his team were upset and I was upset about losing millions of dollars of sales and $250,000 or more in fees for Lamar and me. It was a Saturday and I was planning on returning to Cleveland on Monday but I decided I could field the calls from angry participants just as well from home. I packed up and caught the next plane to Cleveland.

Lamar had protected us by contracting that our agreed 4% commissions would be paid by wire directly to our accounts. We'd grossed $10 million sales from the 40 units. The brokerage sold 11 more units as a direct result of our marketing efforts but Karen wanted not to pay Fisher Auction and my REvision Group for these sales. On a conference call I audited, my friend Dean Adler ripped into her and the whole Related Group.

"Lubert Adler does not screw our sales partners," he growled. "You'll pay them all their earned fees as agreed and negotiated!"

The next day we made the newspapers for conducting what was viewed as a successful auction that "jump started" the Ft Myers downtown residential real estate market. The fact is, it was a pretty successful auction, though we could have sold twice as many condos. For the Related Group, it was regarded as a complete disaster. Poor

Lamar remained upset and disappointed. I was busy trying to digest what I perceived as my own failure.

For the next two years, Related hired various groups to market the Oasis condos but they were never able to generate the excitement or the sales prices that Pérez & Co. thought their condos were worth. Their temper tantrums and unrealistic, irrational behavior the day of our auction cost them millions in lost opportunity. They eventually sold one of the two towers to a Canadian group, who established the units as rentals. In 2014 my friend Greg Fous got the listing, and was still selling units one by one at prices slightly higher than we achieved in 2011.

———————————

I Learn While I Burn: Lesson 7

The worse the experience, the better you learn.

1. *If they don't treat you well, let them go to hell.*
   Of course their friends love them and probably their families do too. But if your deal partners bully you, cheat you, insult you or just smell consistently of bad vibes, walk away. You can do little about their characters, but if you hang around out of greed and/or fear, that's your shortcoming, not theirs.
   Blowing the pop stand is cheaper in the long run because of the opportunity costs entailed in staying. You're sustaining serious wear and tear on your soul when you could instead be thriving with associates who respect you.. I made this fundamental mistake in the Oasis deal and as a result, our hard and effective work was lost.

2. *Never make decisions when your emotions are running high.*
   Well, for once this wasn't my mistake, it was the other guy's —

and I'm looking at you, George Pérez. Of course I can't know what was in his mind at the time — no doubt some complex mix of unrealistic expectations, failure to look at the bigger picture, common-or-garden greed — but I do know that his expensive behavior and rash decision was made at a moment of high anger. He could do nothing to prevent the sale of the first 40 units in an advertised no-reserve auction — he'd already assented to that — but if he'd taken ten minutes to go out for a nice espresso and caught a few deep breaths of fresh air with his team, he'd have allowed the rest of the sale to proceed on the advertised reserve basis. Unfortunately he couldn't because he was busy playing Russian roulette with his blood pressure. Let's admit it, every one of us gets angry sometimes in the face of disappointments. But, You're Majesty, that's no time to start writing your will or signing death warrants!

3. *Don't grab the controls if you don't have your pilot's license.*
At some level, I knew Jon Gollinger's Accelerated Marketing Partners would have been a better strategic partner than my good friend Lamar's Fisher Auction Company. Almost certainly we'd have sold more condos and we'd have had a six-month post-event sales listing. But — and here comes the hard lesson — I wanted control and I knew I'd have more with Lamar than with a bigger sales group like Accelerated. So, as you've read, I got what I wanted.
I was actually to introduce Jon and Lamar to each other in Ft Lauderdale in 2014 and fortunately they both remain good friends of mine. I was to learn that Jon's was one of the other groups that had wanted the Oasis deal and that he was surprised and hurt that I hadn't partnered with him. I think he's still pissed at me for not using his company but even as I write this, he and I are working together in Delray Beach, Florida.

4. *This is a business. Let me see your contract.*
   After all our efforts, elements at Related didn't want to see us paid for our work. And in fact, despite Dean Adler's support, we didn't receive a cent for the post-auction sales. In the first six months after the auction, these sales were a direct result of our marketing and branding efforts.
   Whose fault was that? Ours, of course. Unwritten business agreements are too vulnerable to interpretation after the fact. It's costly and a pain in the ass to have really tight contracts drawn up and agreed to. You've seen the alternative.

5. *Instincts? Use 'em or lose 'em!*
   Decisions can be terribly hard. Despite the advice of smart-alecks, you rarely have the privilege of adding up two columns and going with the higher score. Relying on Lamar's expertise was totally rational: the man had 40 years of auction experience. But I also knew that the absolute no-reserve auction strategy scared the hell out of me and supporting this fear were my dear friends from Related, who tried to convince Lamar that only the first 10 lots should be offered without reserve. Lamar on the other hand and based on his experience, was confident that 40 unreserved lots would produce the highest prices through volume bidding. And who's to say, under the conditions of the time, that he wasn't right? Finally, Lamar knew that with 40 unreserved lots, we'd sell 40 for sure and see our fees for each sale. Wasn't that something we deserved after almost five months' work?
   The argument for calling it from the gut is that our instincts can cut through the rational weighing of options. So if I'd had unfettered control, what would I have done based on what I knew and what I felt? I still don't know. As I say, decisions are difficult.

*

A
BAKKENS
TALE

At 33 years old, Justin Hoff wasn't happy. Raised in Minneapolis, he'd bounced from job to job for years and in 2012 he was dealing blackjack in a Indian-operated casino just outside Madison, Wisconsin. On a slow Tuesday night in the spring of that year, he fell into conversation with a ruddy-faced, moustachioed man in his late forties who had been playing badly but didn't seem much inconvenienced.

"Oh yeah," the man assured Justin when the subject turned to his own life, as it generally did in these circumstances. "Oh yeah. Nobody's never seen nothing like it. Nobody."

Justin dealt his cards. "Where was that?" he asked. It was part of his job to hold up his end of the talk.

"Watford City, North Dakota."

"Never heard of it."

The man chuckled. "Who had? Place is so goddamn bleak, cars

speed up comin' *into* town. I mean, we're talking nowhere, my friend. Dead center."

Justin nodded, looking at the dealt cards. "And you say you're living there because …"

"Because of Bakken, of course." The man had finished his previous whiskey in a single swallow and was looking around for the server.

"Bakken," Justin repeated. He lay down the next round of cards.

"I get the feeling you don't know what I'm talking about, son."

"No, sir. I guess I don't."

The man turned his head to one side and chuckled, as though he had someone beside him who shared the joke.

"The Bakken fields, man. The biggest gold rush since the California days."

Justin looked straight at the fellow for the first time.

"Gold?"

"Black gold, man! Oil! A boom like nobody ever saw. You gotta be kiddin' me that you ain't read nothin' about it."

"I haven't been reading the papers lately."

"Well, that's what you're missing, son."

"So somebody found oil in those fields?"

"Yeah, sorta, about four years ago. But the big companies knew for years there was oil there. It's a ninety-mile stretch — underground shale from Dickinson, North Dakota to Williston, North Dakota. Trouble was, only about one hole in six was a producer — and drilling those damn holes cost eleven million bucks apiece. Companies came and went. It was just too risky."

The casino was almost empty. Justin put down his cards.

"So where did the boom come from?"

"Fracking. You've heard of fracking, right?"

"Sort of."

"Oh boy. You gotta get out more, my friend. Miss! A double Jameson, if you would, please! See, son, the problem in the Bakken is that most of the oil isn't just lyin' underground in pools. It's in the rock

— the shale rock — like water in a sponge. So some smart guy figured out that if you drilled a hole and pumped down a lot of sand and water and chemicals and stuff, you could shatter the hell out of the shale and up would come the oil."

"Wow."

"And some other smart guys figured out how to turn the drill around underground and drill sideways."

"Wow."

"So now, outta every six holes they drill, know how many produce oil?"

"No."

"Six. And you know what the unemployment rate now is in Watford City, North Dakota, right in the middle of the Bakken?"

"No."

"Zero."

Six weeks later, Justin Hoff had quit his job at the casino and driven the 600 miles from Minneapolis to Watford City, North Dakota. There he joined the thousands from all over the U.S. and the world who had flocked to the patch. The Great Recession had wiped out security for many families and a lot of people had nothing to lose, just like the 49ers, 160 years earlier. But most of the 49ers never made a dime, whereas everybody in the Bakken rush made money. There was just one problem.

On his first day in Watford City, Justin got a job in the oil fields that paid three times what he'd been making at the casino. As he stepped out of the company office into the sub-zero North Dakota air, he fell to talking with a skinny kid who also happened to be from Minnesota.

"So where's the best place to stay?" he asked.

His fellow Minnesotan stubbed out his cigarette and immediately lit another.

"Ain't none," he said.

Justin smiled. "So no room in the inn?"

"Ain't no inn," said the kid.

It took Justin about an hour to discover that the few existing hotels were always 100% full. If by chance there was a room, it would be in a ma-and-pa hotel —old, small and dirty. And $375.00 a night if you were lucky.

People just arriving would drive fifty miles in the snow and cold to get a room. At 10:00 p.m. two armed security guards at the Walmart in nearby Williston would open its gates and allow 1400 cars and trucks to come in so people could sleep in them. North Dakota had become the fastest growing state in the Union and the population was increasing by 9% a month as recession-weary oil workers — or would-be oil workers — saw their chance to get back on their feet. Minimum wage that year was $6.65. In places like Williston and Watford City, McDonald's was offering $14.00 an hour and a $200 signing bonus.

For six weeks, Justin slept in his car. Then, as a muddy North Dakota spring was getting underway, he made friends with Craig Nelson, a Watford City cement yard owner, and Craig and his wife took Justin into their home, where he stayed for the next six months. He was getting $52.00 an hour and could put in as many hours and as much overtime as he wanted. He'd never worked that hard and he'd never made that much money. His appetite for opportunity had been whetted, however, and it was clear where the opportunity lay. Together, he and Craig purchased sixty acres as a site for future housing. Neither of them had any development experience but Craig had grown up in Watford City City, as had his parents, and he knew everybody in town. All the new partners needed was money.

In 2012, John Askew, who'd worked with me in New York at the new Champions Basketball League, introduced me to a fellow from North

Dakota named Joel Rosen, who was looking for backing for a new multi-level merchandising venture. I listened politely to Joel's pitch but I had a pretty well-established suspicion of multi-level businesses. We chatted for a bit afterwards though, and he told me about his best friend, a young guy named Justin Hoff, a former Minnesota casino employee who was trying to develop housing in Watford City, North Dakota. Apparently there was something going on there called the Bakken Oil Boom.

"Save your breath, Joel." I actually laughed. "I hate winter. I'd never ever get involved in any deal in some place like North Dakota."

The matter rested there for a week or so, until one afternoon I got a call from Justin Hoff himself. I listened because I liked the guy's enthusiasm, but afterwards I went online and looked up Watford City. Sure enough. It was cold, ugly and hard to get to.

It's difficult to say what really goes on in entrepreneurial minds like mine, but over the next week I found myself thinking about Watford City. Maybe it was the challenge. "Where's there's muck, there's money," as I remembered people saying. Then Justin Hoff called again.

"Alright, alright," I told him. "I'm coming."

In November of 2012, I flew from Cleveland to Denver. From Denver there was one flight to Williston ND, a little Beechcraft 1900 turboprop operated by an outfit called Great Lakes Airlines. "They call it Great Shakes," the booking agent told me with a humourless smile.

In the Denver waiting area, I met Jeff from Louisiana. He'd been working steady at home but couldn't get out of debt and his wife and kids had all encouraged him to head north to the Bakken fields. He was to report to a "man camp" and he was scared about what might await him there, to say nothing of the long hours.

"I jes' heard them say it's 13 degrees without that there wind chill factor," he told me, pretty quiet. "I don't know. We ain't got no wind chill in Baton Rouge."

Jeff went off to the washroom and I started talking with Chris from Amarillo, Texas. He was tall and he was actually wearing an expensive-looking cowboy hat.

"Yep," he drawled, "I'm a tech on a big rig and this is my third commute this quarter. Generally I work eighteen straight days, then get eight days off."

"Wow."

"'Course I get a lotta overtime and triple time sometimes 'cause we operate 24/7. Sometimes I'll work 24/30 hours straight, then go back to my place and sleep and eat and get up and do it again."

"Wow," I marvelled. "I doubt the millennials would go for that work/life balance."

"Who's that?" Chris asked.

I got aboard to find the cabin full, the small seats crammed with big guys. The cost for the one hour and 21 minute flight was $750.00. This was my introduction to what the word "boom" might mean.

I stepped onto the tarmac at Sloulin Field International Airport, Williston N.D. and saw that it was small and ugly. I had no idea then that the facility was slated to be shuttered and totally replaced as the boom continued. All I could see was that nobody was smiling and there were hardly any women and some of those looked like men. I rented a little SUV and set off for Watford City, about an hour away. I was almost immediately overwhelmed by a flood of speeding trucks. I had never seen so many crammed onto one highway and my vehicle felt awfully small in the roaring horde. On either side there were tall oil rigs, their tops flaming against the darkening sky. I felt like I was an extra in a movie — science fiction or horror, I wasn't sure.

So here was my opportunity. Thousands of oil workers were coming to town every month. Justin and Craig had recognized that if they could buy cheap land and get it zoned and licensed for housing, they could make a fortune. Justin had designed cabins that could be made in a pre-fab warehouse and trucked to North Dakota from Minnesota and Montana. They could get $3000 a month for a 254-square-foot cabin but they needed real estate experience and more importantly they needed investors.

I joined Justin and Craig as a partner and started commuting to North Dakota every week. I needed to understand the demographics and I needed to meet all the players. At the time I was working with a few capital groups in NYC and one of these was John Domo, a personal acquaintance and a successful developer from Cleveland who was then living in New York and trying to produce a play on Broadway. We agreed to meet for lunch at Sara Jane's and there I recounted the tale of the Bakken oil boom and the desperate housing shortage. John was intrigued and told me he'd bring in the money if what I said was true. Before the lunch was over we'd sketched out our deal on a Sara Jane napkin.

"We'll draw up a formal agreement after I see this place," he said. We agreed to fly the following week to the Bakken patch. We shook hands and I eyed his Emporio Armani suit, his Rolex, his Quaranta Locatelli tie.

"Er, John," I said, not wanting to chill the mood. "By the way. Probably better if you bring a different wardrobe to North Dakota."

"Why's that?" He frowned. "What's the matter with my wardrobe?"

"Nothing. It's totally great. But we'll be going to a wildcatter town and, you know, lotta oil workers and like that."

"So what do they wear?" John demanded.

He did travel in outdoor gear — brand new outdoor gear — but it didn't protect him from the psychological shock of brutal cold and brutal scenery. We fought our way across the snow-swept tarmac to the little Williston terminal.

"Christ, Mike," he yelled above the wind. "I just remembered I left my fountain pen on my desk in New York. I'll be back."

"Hang on, John," I called. "We're talking money here, not suntans."

"Maybe just this once I might go for the suntan?"

"Yeah, but remember, here we're never gonna get burned!" I yelled.

Fateful words.

John quickly came in as our investor partner and as promised, he produced an agreement. It was about twenty pages and I didn't want him to know I couldn't afford a lawyer.

"Great," I said.

As our capital partner, he took control. We purchased seventy more acres and began to build our own cabins. We called the development the Grand Bakken Lodge and started negotiating with oil companies that wanted to give us one- or two-year leases for as many cabins as we could build. Our rental price was $3000 a month and our total cost per unit was about $52,000, fully furnished. We'd have our capital back in less than two years.

The boom rolled on. It wasn't just oil production that was flourishing. Restaurants, hardware stores, hotels, strip clubs — every conceivable accoutrement of civilization was rushing to this middle of nowhere. I myself commuted back and forth every week from Ohio and Florida, where I had other real estate deals in progress. After a while I realized I was getting lonely and starting to wear at the edges. I struggled a bit to keep my focus on the possibility of owning hundreds or maybe thousands of these rental units. John didn't seem to have time to make the trip and he and Justin weren't getting along at all.

"I gotta lot going on here in New York, Mike," he explained. "I mean, I've got a big show going to Broadway."

"I know. That's great, John. It's just quite a lot of work we're trying to get done in the Bakkens."

"Yeah, Mike. But you've got Justin and those guys out there. And I am letting you draw an advance, right?"

"Yes. I'm really grateful for that, John. As a matter of fact, I think you were going to send an installment this month."

"Oh yeah? You haven't got it?"

"Well, not yet."

"Oh yeah? I'll check that out, Mike. And listen, Mike. I know you're sourcing capital for other people's deals. Think you could source some more for us?"

"Um. Me?"

"Yeah. Howzabout tapping a few of those sources for us?"

"I … I thought you were gonna be doing that, John?"

"I am, Mike. Sure I am. But everybody's gotta pull their weight, right?"

"Yeah. Right, I guess."

"And remember, Mike, it's me's got control in this deal."

"I thought we were partners, John."

"We are, bud. Sure we are. But look at your contract."

True to my nature, I was meanwhile networking with everybody in town. My initial role in arranging the financing for our housing development seemed to have established my niche. Traditional banks were hesitant to provide funding, so when a Bakken developer or broker was trying to put a deal together, guys started calling me up to ask if I could help bring in private equity.

After his first visit, John stopped showing up in North Dakota altogether and his operating cash — and my advances — gradually dried up. Creditors were pretty soon howling louder than a northern prairie wind. The Grand Bakken Lodge project was in trouble and I didn't have enough funds of my own to grow as a developer — nor, it occurred to me, the desire. I reflected instead that, "when one door closes, another opens." I seized that door handle and created a new company and called it Bakken Strategic Marketing. Why couldn't I be the go-to guy for everybody who needed funding for their businesses? As it turned out, I could. I brought in KKR, the first Wall Street group to put serious money into the Bakkens, and this gave me huge credibility. From there I ultimately raised about 23 million dollars from three different New York capital sources and helped construct two apartment buildings and a strip mall.

The blush was coming off the Grand Bakken Lodge rose. John was fighting with Justin by phone and I was trying to act as referee, but actually sympathetic to Justin, whom I liked and trusted. For a while John filled the cash gaps by borrowing from new investors and thus diluting Justin and me. We were having some minor title issues with the municipality and some more than minor credit issues with our contractors.

"That's your baby, Mikey," John told me. "You handle it. I got other fish to fry."

Handle it I did and three years later John's investors got title to the property they'd invested in. Long before that, though, I'd been called into the offices of John's lawyers and told that my equity in the venture had evaporated.

"It was your drawdowns, Mr Friedman," a balding kid explained. "You've already had your share. Check your contract."

"But I owned twenty-five per cent of the project," I protested.

"Not any more you don't, Mr Friedman."

"And what about the $85,000 dollars John owes me?"

"You'll have to talk that over with Mr Domo."

As my second North Dakota winter dragged on, business associates were tempting me with opportunities in Florida and Colorado. Thoughts of strolling to meetings in a short-sleeve shirt were starting to haunt me at night. It was costing me close to $1000 to fly out to the

Bakken region and the crummy little hotels would normally charge me between $300 and $500 a night. The beauty of supply and demand seemed less beautiful when I was on the demand side and this all came to a head when I arrived in Williston one afternoon in February 2014.

It was thirty-eight below zero Fahrenheit. My rental car was waiting for me but nobody had thought to let it warm up. I had twenty-five minutes to get to my first meeting at the Williston Brewing Company, which had just opened to supply beer to all the workers in the area. It was about a ten minute drive from the airport but by the time I'd got organized, I just had time to make it to the brewery, where my clients were waiting. I pulled up with one minute to spare, switched off the ignition, and grabbed my briefcase, yanked on the door handle. Nothing. After several desperate tries, I crawled into the back seat but the back doors were frozen too. I banged frantically on the windows but no one was loitering outside Williston Brewery. Abject with embarrassment, I called my clients from my cell phone. Fifteen minutes and four large pots of boiling water later, I emerged from my car with a sheepish grin to reclaim my day.

That night, I left my car in the parking lot of the hotel. I remember vaguely wondering why all the trucks were empty but running. This was clarified the next morning when I came out to find my windows encased in six inches of solid ice. In Ohio, an ice scraper would have solved this, so for half an hour I provided entertainment for a gaggle of idle and callous individuals who watched me, my fingers frozen and my eyebrows sprouting glaciers, as I chopped and chipped with my plastic tool. Finally, some humanitarian called out a truck driver and hotel staffer, who used boiling water in conjunction with hammer and chisel. I noted with grim satisfaction that it took them twenty-five minutes.

My Bakken adventure was over.

Fallout

Five weeks after I returned to Cleveland in 2014, done with the Bakken for good, the price of oil began its collapse. In less than two months, I went from $112 a barrel to $39 a barrel. Some of the deals I helped put together held — the Bakken boom has continued at a less hectic level — and some got killed. On balance I was one of the lucky ones who got the timing right and made good money.

Justin Hoff never went back to dealing at the blackjack tables but did go on to found other companies in North Dakota. He has married and commutes from his home in Wisconsin to North Dakota. John Domo continued to raise capital for Broadway productions. In 2013 he was a producer of the musical Big Fish. One of my clients invested in the production and lost $850,000 in three months.

Grand Bakken Lodge was sold.

CRAIN'S CLEVELAND BUSINESS

August 29, 2014 02:30 AM

GO WEST, FRIEDMAN!

While a lot of Ohioans were waiting for drilling to take off in the Utica shale, Beachwood resident Michael Friedman already was cashing in on the new boom in high-volume, slick-water, horizontal drilling and hydraulic fracturing, or fracking, as it's commonly known.
He just had to go to North Dakota to do it.

Friedman has been working the big Bakken shale play in the Dakotas, and he said he's finding more opportunities as he expands the scope of his activities. While Friedman originally focused on building and renting out housing for oilfield workers, he's now also brokering deals and arranging financing for other developers in the region.

"Three years ago, I went to the Bakken on a referral to help a friend raise some money to do a residential development," Friedman said. "We ended up buying it and calling it the Grand Bakken Lodge. That was the start of my career there."

If Friedman's name sounds familiar, there's good reason. He's known to hard-core area sports fans and pizza connoisseurs alike, first for his stint as a basketball coach at Case Western Reserve University and Dyke College in the 1980s, and then for his ownership of several Captain Tony's pizza shops in and around Cleveland.

CRAIN'S CLEVELAND BUSINESS

But he says nothing has kept him as busy as the Bakken shale.

Friedman's Grand Bakken Lodge turned into a 30-unit housing development for oilfield workers. While it's not a Ritz-Carlton — or even a luxury apartment complex, by most standards — it was a far cry from and leagues above the so-called "man camps" available to many rig workers.

Instead of the barracks-style living of the man camps, where sometimes dozens of workers roomed together under a single roof, Grand Bakken offered individual, 300-square-foot cabins with their own kitchens, laundry facilities, bathrooms and sleeping quarters.

1,300 to 13,000

Friedman said his plan was to expand the project to 800 units. He secured $30 million in financing in 2011 from New York investors and lease commitments from North Dakota drillers, but then his partners got cold feet and the deal was abandoned.

But Friedman had been bitten; the Bakken was too big and too good an opportunity to turn away from, he said. And he'd already learned an awful lot about the needs of oil and gas drillers, and how to capitalize on those needs in North Dakota.

First, he saw the demand for housing first hand, as he watched the town of Watford City, N.D., struggle to cope with the rapid influx of new oil rig workers.

"When I started (in 2012), Watford City had 1,300 residents," Friedman said. "Now they're up to 13,000."

CRAIN'S CLEVELAND BUSINESS

Oil workers fill every hotel for a hundred miles or more, he said, even though the nightly rates have risen to $175. Others fill the man camps, while the most unlucky often sleep in their cars in a Wal-Mart parking lot, specially set up for that purpose at night.

"About 2,500 people a night would line up at 10:30," he said. "They'd let 2,500 cars in and they would sleep there."

He also learned that oil companies were willing to pay for housing, they just couldn't find it.

"We had tremendous demand," Friedman said. "Hess Oil had a terrific need for housing and they couldn't fill it. All of the oil companies became tired of their people staying in man camps. It's a terrible quality of life."

Hitting the ATM

So, when Friedman offered Hess cabins for its workers — even at $3,000 a month in rent for a small unit — they didn't balk, or even blink.

Then, he learned how profitable it all could be.

It cost about $50,000 to build, haul in, furnish and set up a pre-fabricated cabin, Friedman said. But, at the $3,000-a-month rent level, they pay for themselves in about 18 months.

"After that, it's just like going to the ATM every month," said Friedman, who added that while the generally young workers did put some wear and tear on the units, it was minimal compared to his revenues.

CRAIN'S CLEVELAND BUSINESS

Friedman also learned something that his strength in the region was being able to network with oil companies working in the shale, developers looking for ways to finance their shale-related projects, and out-of-state investors looking for a way to put their money into the nation's shale boom.

So Friedman kept his 30 units and his deal with Hess, sold off the 80 acres he had set aside for more units, and started looking for opportunities as a deal broker.

Now, he said he raises millions for other housing and commercial developments in the region, usually tapping hedge funds and family investment groups from New York, Philadelphia and California. Friedman continues to cultivate new clients, including drilling companies looking for housing and developers looking for finance, real estate, or both.

One such developer has been Paul Dries of Louisville, Ky., who now spends about three weeks per month in North Dakota working on real estate developments. His company, Bakken Development Solutions, specializes in buying land and preparing it for commercial development by installing water, sewage, electrical lines and, in some cases, even roads. He's found both buyers and financing through Friedman, he said.

"Mike has been an important source of introduction to various people in the region for us," Dries said. "He has done a good job of creating relationships within the Bakken, and then taking the relationships he has formed over the years in his real estate endeavors and connecting people who might have like-minded interests."

For example, when Dries had for sale a 20-acre site in Watford City that was ready for development, Friedman introduced him to

CRAIN'S CLEVELAND BUSINESS

a multifamily real estate development company that was looking for a place to build. Dries sold them the property, which now is the site of more than 300 new housing units, he said.

Most everyone knows his name

According to Dries, Friedman is part real estate agent, part dealmaker and part local celebrity — at least among the highly interconnected drilling and development crowd.

"If you went into a restaurant (in Watford City), there is a good chance that someone is in that restaurant that Mike would know," Dries said. "Maybe more than one, maybe four or five — but there would be at least one."

Friedman said he gets a commission on each sale he helps set up or each round of financing he facilitates. He also gets a small ownership stake in most of the real estate transactions he shepherds.

While he won't disclose what he's making from the work, Friedman said it's the best business opportunity he's ever found. He also says it's not about to end anytime soon, which is one reason he's willing to be paid, in part, with small equity positions in Bakken developments.

"They say they'll need 79,000 wells to fully tap the Bakken, and they have 6,000 wells drilled so far," Friedman said. "You do the math. ... This so-called 'boom' is not going to be over anytime soon, probably not in my lifetime."

Published by permission of Crain's Cleveland Business

I Learn While I Burn: Lesson 8

Experience is a hard teacher but she never retires.

Alright, I made money in the Bakken oil fields. But I didn't make it in quite the way I'd planned, so it still counts as a flesh wound. What can I say about the whole, chilly episode?

First, I lacked confidence and experience so I shared all my info with John Domo. John had the experience and leverage and he represented that he had the capital so Justin and I made him a partner. We never executed an official agreement and I had nowhere to turn when he asked me for help with the fund-raising. From there, the ride was downhill.

Were there take-aways? Sure. There are always take-aways.

Trust your instincts and don't let greed or lack of confidence in your own abilities tempt you to join up with people that you don't like or trust.

Always get proper legal advice and have legal documentation with buy/sell agreements, and a working operating agreement.

However unlikely, shit happens. Oil prices can crash, your partner can screw you, meetings can be called when it's 40 degrees below zero and your car's windows are frozen. Keep a few options in your back pocket.

Most important, face up immediately when there are problems with other people. The reputation you save may be your own and come in mighty handy when a sudden pivot in a new direction becomes necessary.

*

THE DEAL
TO A
KEY

If you've followed me to here — our last chapter — you'll have appreciated that I advanced along my career path — no, my *paths* — through a combination of good calls and bad calls. I'm confident this is how anyone who is still standing when the music stops manages to go forward in a competitive environment. If success could be guaranteed by learning some simple lesson — some "secret" — then everyone would learn that lesson and no one would gain any advantage. But in fact lessons are learned through hard individual experience and not everyone is equipped to stay the course and reap the benefits.

A corollary to this is the fact that most large real estate deals are highly complex, not basic transactions such as buying a bag of potatoes. You'll remember how Captain Tony's Gourmet Pizza was hard but straightforward work, yet even that that was only true after the risky business of finding the initial capital. Once I set off into the realm of bigger business, I entered a world in which many players participate, each bringing their own characters, needs, fears and styles. That's why most project developments look like the inside of a Swiss watch. I've had to be somewhat sketchy about details throughout this book because if I'd described anything like a complete catalogue of my ventures — or almost ventures — I'd have lost you at the start.

At this point, however, my life entered a phase in which the many years' painful stumbles — and moderate successes — had begun to bear fruit. I'd maintained a host of relationships — what's usually called a "network" — that continued to grow. These relationships are the invisible threads that tie together any cooperative enterprise. If you're on the outside, you might sneer at them as an "old boys' network." But of course "new boys" are allowed to enter or there soon wouldn't be a network. It takes time though to grow a network, just as a gardener's main virtue is his patience.

Having said all that, I hope you'll stay with me for a few pages more as we dissect one last deal — among the bigger ones in my experience — and decide for yourself what made it go the way it did.

A dreary, rainy day in November, 2014 and Frank and I were driving through downtown Cleveland. He was starting to think seriously about moving the offices from the suburbs. As we drove by Public Square, we passed the Key Tower and he craned his neck to look up at its 57 stories.

"Hey, Mike," he said. "Why don't we take a run at that one?"

It had been a year since I'd wound down my Bakken adventure and six months since a friend had introduced me to Frank Sinito, CEO of the Millennia Companies Group, headquartered in Cleveland. In the "affordable real estate" class, Frank was one of the most successful and powerful developers in the U.S. When we met we'd agreed that I'd introduce him to some of my NYC equity investors and this led to my arranging a $75 million loan for his company. I received my fee and walked away happy.

Except that, months later, Frank invited me for lunch and during that lunch he surprised me by bringing up the idea of my taking over as head of Millennia Housing Capital, the company's financing division. I was involved in another venture entirely at the time and wasn't especially enthusiastic about becoming an employee again. Frank, however, was a persuasive man. He invited me to accompany him and a few other Millennia people on a trip to Oklahoma and points west. We flew in the company jet and touched down three or four times to inspect a number of their properties. I was blown away by his team's dedication and work ethic though in the end it was the prospect of going out into the capital market to represent such a respected sponsor as Millennia that persuaded me.

"Really." Frank was still looking up at the Tower. "Why don't we take a run at it?"

"Sure," I chuckled.

"Do some research?"

"Sure."

Key Tower had been designed by architect César Pelli and built in the early 1990s. It was the tallest building between New York and Chicago and was owned by Columbia, an Atlanta-based REIT that was offering it for sale. The broker was investment bankers Eastdil Secured. I knew Frank wasn't delusional so I assumed he was kidding but a year passed

and he was more adamant than ever that we had to move downtown. Then, about that time, I learned that Scott Wolstein, from a well- known Cleveland real estate family, wanted to meet with Frank. Apparently he'd just taken control of Key Tower and hoped that Millennia would be a tenant. Scott and Frank met at Frank's house and drank a few bottles of wine and had a gourmet dinner. Frank made it clear that he'd love to move his company to Key Tower, but would need to own some of the building. He owned 23,900 apartment units at the time and wasn't in the habit of renting. Frank and I traveled to NYC to meet with the CEO of Emigrant Bank and came out of the meeting feeling that we might be the better lead developer. We returned to Cleveland to discover that Scott had lost control of the deal.

The new lead buyer was American Landmark, a large real estate investor out of Chicago. They currently owned two office buildings in Cleveland but a Cleveland buddy of mine was their lead guy in town. So Frank was out a few bottles of wine but we might still be in the game.

I told my buddy of our desire to be a partner in the acquisition and he told me that if we could make a $5 million investment, we could move into about 30,000 square feet as tenants. That seemed worth discussing but negotiations crawled along and we were getting nowhere. I decided to bypass Landmark and go directly to Eastdil Secured, the broker. Eastdil told me that American Landmark had failed so far to put down the necessary deposit. The letter of intent had expired. Key Tower was back on the market.

"Wow." I could feel my heart speeding up a little. "Okay, so what would Millennia have to do to put our hat in the ring as a potential buyer?"

"Look, Mike." The Eastdil guy put down the pen he'd been holding. "The owners at Columbia are pissed that both Wolstein and American Landmark have crapped out. They'd be really reluctant to entertain an offer from a little outfit like Millennia to buy such a large building."

"Still, there has to be a price …"

"Yeah, but it's $310 million dollars now."

Frank and I talked it over and he gave me full authority to try to negotiate with Eastdil to see if the owners would meet with us and entertain an offer. Our sales pitch was simple: we lived in Cleveland, we were going to be a large tenant of the building, we knew how to manage assets, we had hospitality experience. The building was being sold with an underground garage and a Marriott Hotel. Our consultants urged us to sell the hotel because managing a hotel was tough. Frank refused any advice and kept his focus on the entire package.

We clearly faced huge hurdles if we were going to be accepted as serious buyers. For four weeks straight, I called the brokers at Eastdil and the brokers tried to divert our interest to other office buildings in Cleveland. Columbia, they insisted, couldn't afford another group backing out. They were a public REIT and their stockholders were getting antsy.

"Okay," I told Frank. "I'm going to call Columbia directly, and bypass the damn broker." He agreed it couldn't hurt at this point. The V.P. of Columbia, however, told me that we didn't have a big enough bank balance. They were looking for a larger and more experienced buyer. Sorry. Thanks.

The next time Eastdil called me, I put the "takeaway" strategy into play.

"I'm sorry," I said. "We're busy here and I don't want to speak to you people anymore. If you do want to speak to me again, please have some positive news about Key Tower. Sorry. Thanks."

Three days later, they called me and said they wanted to coordinate a call with Columbia and Frank and me. The call went well, but the COO at Columbia kept insisting that if we wanted them to take us seriously and move to a letter of intent (LOI) we'd have to make an offer close to 300 million with a short due diligence period and a "hard non-refundable deposit." We were mulling all that over when they called us and said they'd reconsidered and didn't want to waste their time or ours. Sheesh.

The next day I called Richie Horwitz, the principal at NYC investment bank Cooper-Horwitz. Richie was convinced he could put together one or more groups able to provide the debt and help with the equity. (If you happen to be unfamiliar with financing terms, "debt" financing is essentially a loan and "equity" financing is the purchase by the financing party of a share of the company or project in question.) We made another call to the president of Columbia and told him about Cooper-Horwitz. My real message was that we wouldn't be brushed away.

"Okay, fine," he said. "Please send us your offer."

We submitted our first LOI for $250 million. Needless to say, this offer didn't have them weeping for joy but we had good data and compelling arguments that it was a fair offer. They asked for $5 million hard cash deposit and we agreed. This was enormously risky for Frank but we were determined and had to demonstrate our seriousness. We negotiated through our respective lawyers and eventually got them to agree on a $267 million sales price. It was touching to see how excited and honored Frank was to be considered a buyer. The closing date on the contract was December 1st, 2016.

The hard part began. We had to find the money.

Early April, 2016: 270 days to December 1st 2016 closing.

I put together a list of all the equity groups we would contact, including a few investment bankers I'd been working with. We decided to have two brokerages compete for the debt: Cooper-Horwitz and a local guy, Mark Vogel, who ran Berkadia. I had each of them submit a list of 25 banks/funds that they would like to target and I assured that they could not go after one another's list. Neither broker liked this method, but it was best for Millennia. Frank and I meanwhile decided it was time for me to become a consultant rather than a full-time employee; this would allow me to collect a proper fee for putting together the financing.

The competition between the two brokerages was intense, each accusing the other of attempted circumvention. We had them make their presentation, and we ended up moving forward with Cooper-Horwitz, who lined up Morgan Stanley from NYC, who put together a strong, non-recourse, low-interest debt deal for up to $250 million of the $267 million sale. Of course, with the closing and legal fees and some tenant improvement costs, we were looking at a total cost of about $315 to $320 million.

To get our equity raising efforts underway I conducted seminars and webinars. I invited groups to tour Key Tower with Frank and people from the Jacobs Real Estate Group, who had been managing and leasing the building since their boss Dick Jacobs built it in 1991. Our goal was about $20 to $25 million, mostly from wealthy individuals — some of my Millennia investors and some of my personal contacts . It was going pretty well: I'd raised about $11 million. Our investor package was designed so that Frank would own the majority of the building after ten years and the investors would realize a strong return on their investment, get all their capital back, and still own a small share of the building in perpetuity.

135 days to December 1st 2016 closing.

Through my Cleveland contacts, I learned that Forest City, the largest and oldest real estate company in the city, was thinking about selling their building and constructing new premises or becoming a tenant in a triple-A office building. What could be more triple-A than Key Tower? I called my buddy Chandler Converse who confirmed he was representing Forest City. Frank and I invited Chandler to Frank's summer club The Bratenhall and took him on Frank's boat down Lake Erie to the city. There was Key Tower, rising above the waterfront. How could Forest City resist?

We were buying the building with a current occupancy rate of 83%. With Millennia and Berkadia and possibly Forest City moving in, we would be close to 94%. The bad news was that we would need some $17 million more in equity. On top of the $16 million I was still short, I was now $33 million short. We had two months left to close and Frank was getting nervous. He'd risked a significant non-refundable down payment and another non-refundable deposit was due if we wanted to move forward. We worked twelve hours every day.

82 days to December 1st 2016 closing.

Then it happened. Morgan Stanley backed out of the deal. Mark Vogel of Berkadia, who'd lost out to Morgan Stanley, had predicted this and warned us. Frank, absolutely furious, swung into a crisis mode, called Berkadia and persuaded Mark and his partner to come back on board. Mark and company responded brilliantly and got their original capital guys to come in and give us a new LOI within four days. Unfortunately the new terms were much worse for Millennia.

Our debt challenges were resolved but our equity shortfall was keeping me awake at night. We needed about $18 million in equity and if Forest City signed a lease, we'd need another $15 million or so to build out their offices. I was literally working around the clock. We set up meetings with big equity groups across the USA and Canada. Baupost of Boston sent in an analyst to do their own underwriting. Skyline, a large hotel developer from Toronto, loved the hotel and was willing to provide some much needed equity for the Tower provided Frank would sell the hotel outright to them. I liked the idea but Frank refused to consider it.

Meanwhile, during the whole seven months of the Key Tower scramble, my great friend Dean Adler had been conspicuously unenthusiastic about the merits of the Key acquisition for Frank and Millennia. Now, with the clock ticking, he unexpectedly began to get excited. Certainly he knew a successful transaction would help me out but I believe he was genuinely exploring whether this deal could work for his fund, Adler, perhaps in a co-venture with Baupost. After some indecision, he decided it would make more sense for Lubert Adler to do the deal alone. Now we were all excited. We made another hard down payment for an extension to January 29th 2017.

15th January, 2017: 14 days to January 29th 2017 closing.

New taxes suddenly reared up that we hadn't accounted for. Our lenders re-traded the deal and demanded more from Frank and his debt service coverage ratio. Meanwhile I began collecting the money from the investors who had already committed and lo! they had a ton of new questions and new apprehensions. Lubert Adler also was having second thoughts and asked for some guaranteed returns that would hurt the overall equity of the deal. We decided the only way to satisfy Adler and keep the current equity investors whole was to have Frank subordinate all his returns and fees to Lubert Adler and spare the other investors any effect.

17th January, 2017: 12 days to January 29th 2017 closing,

I thought we were home free, but every day was bringing new issues. It was wearing on Frank, and he was understandably stressed and nervous, with millions of his own money on the line. I decided, based on my years of leading teams and overcoming adversity, I'd tell Frank in a nice way to get his head out of his ass and stop moping. He was our leader and he had to put on a positive front. I'm not sure Frank appreciated my pep talk but after the closing, he was gracious enough to thank me.

20th January, 2017: 9 days to January 29th 2017 closing.

We were still short about $15 million and Adler would not help out further. They suggested instead that we go to the seller and ask for a reduced sales price. The theory was that we were pretty close and Columbia had already announced the sale to their shareholders. Surely they wouldn't want another last minute bust. Frank was totally not interested in new negotiations with the seller but Dean thought it was stupid not to try. I was the middle man and after discussing the strategy with Frank I approached the broker, who duly approached the CEO of Columbia. He flat out turned us down.

22nd January, 2017: 7 days to January 29th 2017 closing.

Dean Adler came through again. His partner in Atlanta, Neil Faucet, had a golf buddy who was on the Columbia board. We begged Frank to go down to Atlanta and meet with Neil. He was hesitant and nervous about taking this trip, but we insisted. I received a call two nights later.

"Hey. Mike. I loved meeting this guy Neil!"

"That's great, Frank!"

"Yeah, we bonded right off."

"Fabulous! I knew they liked us."

"Well, not exactly. But it turns out Neil and I are both born-again Christians."

"Er … that's good, right, Frank?"

"Of course it's good! By the end of the evening, we were discussing a carry back of $12 million from Columbia! They're basically lending us the money we'll be paying them."

"Praise the lord, Frank!"

"What?"

"Praise the lord!"

"Hey, Mike. You're a Jew."

"Just one God, Frank, and it sounds to me like he's on our side."

"You're right, brother."

28th January, 2017: 36 hours to January 29th closing.

Both lenders and Lubert Adler had some last minute problems and requested we delay the closing date. We contacted Columbia. They said they wouldn't honor the $12 million deferment if we didn't close by the deadline and our deposits would be forfeit. They did however agree to extend the closing date to 30th January.

10 a.m. 30th January, 2017: 14 hours to January 30th 2017 closing.

Lubert Adler called. They demanded that we look at the numbers. They said we were $3 million short and they needed Frank to pony it up in cash immediately. Also they'd prefer a new closing date in February. "You're making a mistake," we said. Frank and the whole team freaked out.

12 p.m. 30th January, 2017: 12 hours to January 30th closing deadline.

Lubert Adler accountants called. They agreed they'd made a mistake in their calculations.

1:30 p.m. 30th January, 2017.

We closed the Key Tower purchase. It was the biggest deal in the city in several years and the biggest deal in Millennia's history. We currently have our offices in Key Tower and we're over 95% occupied. Our investors and Lubert Adler have enjoyed excellent returns.

10:00 p.m. 30th January, 2017.

We had a hell of a party at Frank's. The next day I left for Delray Beach for a month.

AFTERWORD

I mentioned this at the start but I have to say it again. After almost fifty years in the working world, I've arrived at the conviction that I've learned a few useful things about that world. I haven't set them out in this little book as organized principles such as you might learn in school. You've probably noticed, as I have, that life isn't really like that. But I thought that following a few of my hits and misses might be a help to some of my readers.

I've observed, for instance, how the successful coach or businessperson or employee or parent or anyone entering the working world all share certain characteristics. They focus on their goals, they develop a passion for what they do, and they develop habits that continually build on their expertise. They master the simple fundamentals of their craft, develop confidence by overcoming the consequences of their mistakes and by winning small victories.

Perhaps my most important revelation is how I — and maybe you — can carry a set of personal skills from one endeavour to another. Failures allow us draw the map that let's us navigate better through the next challenge/career.

It almost goes without saying that our connections to other people is central to any undertaking. I've had many people who doubted me and some who supported me. But I've tried never to shut a door I could leave open and the building of "human capital" has been the key to my growth. Not only do human relationships developed through jobs and social networks add richness to our quality of life, they also comprise of true investment. I may move from one business sphere to another, but many of the same relationships emerge again and again to aid my enterprise.

If you're reading this, I know you'll appreciate that I don't expect you to be like me. I've changed careers over and over again as opportunities presented themselves. You on the other hand might find satisfaction in a single field. Although I've worked for largish companies, I've discovered I'm happiest depending on myself. You on the other hand may have found your place through a long-term commitment to one organization. But whatever the differences between us, we'll both learn through mistakes and both progress through small successes that build confidence in ourselves.

As I write, I still hold the position of president of Millennia Housing Capital, with whom I worked on the acquisition of the Key Tower. I've raised over $220 million for Millennia's acquisitions of affordable multi-family developments.

Here I'm addressing 650 employees as keynote speaker at Millennia's annual conference in Cleveland, Ohio. I recall my theme was the company's mission and why it was so exciting to work for it. Whether I got them with my humor or my enthusiasm, something inspired a rousing standing ovation.

I'm also building my own company, the REvision Group, which helps source capital for sponsors of real estate developments. I identify the best developers and create joint venture limited partnerships with my connections in the equity world. I have three "buckets" of investors: private equity, family offices, and wealthy individual funds. The human capital I've built through twenty-year relationships with these people and institutions give me the credibility to introduce opportunities and create deal flow for both the parties. In the process I create a revenue stream for the REvision Group.

In the last two years, I've started a public speaking program to help small and medium-size businesses with their sales teams, and advise them in their recruitment and retention of employees. I've also been speaking to people who want to "recreate" themselves by starting their own businesses or changing their careers. I meanwhile partner up with the Boys and Girls Clubs around the USA, giving a free basketball clinic in every city where I do a presentation.

January 2019. I direct a free basketball clinic for the Boys and Girls Club in Cleveland and in cities around the USA.

My current plan is to work until I'm eighty years old, building both the REvision Group and Mike Talks, and then sit down with Sindi and the boys and have a serious discussion about whether I should push on to one hundred. As usual, we'll resolve this by democratic vote.

* * *

You can reach me for speaking engagements at 216-214-2668

I raise capital for the Millennia Companies at http://www.mhmltd.com

I operate my own capital-sourcing company, The REvision Group. You can find us at http://www.TheREvisionGroup.com

Find my public speaking venture, Mike Talks, at http://www.MikeTalks.life

Every morning I send out a "Great Morning" quote to some 350 people. They start our day in a positive way and if you'd like to join us, write me at Mjfgogetter@yahoo.com and put in the subject line, "Please send Great Morning quotes."

Good luck in your own journey!

Mike

www.ingramcontent.com/pod-product-compliance
Lightning Source LLC
Chambersburg PA
CBHW021324060726
47591CB00006B/1852